SERVANT-LEAD

For a complete list of Management Books 2000 titles
visit our web-site on http://www.mb2000.com

SERVANT-LEADERSHIP
Bringing the Spirit of Work to Work

Edited by
Ralph Lewis and John Noble

2000

First published in 2008 by Management Books 2000 Ltd
Forge House, Limes Road
Kemble, Cirencester
Gloucestershire, GL7 6AD, UK
Tel: 0044 (0) 1285 771441
Fax: 0044 (0) 1285 771055
Email: info@mb2000.com
Web: www.mb2000.com

British Library Cataloguing in Publication Data is available

ISBN 9781852525712

Robert K Greenleaf (1904 – 1990)

Contents

Contents

Acknowledgements

The Greenleaf Centre for Servant-Leadership UK (Greenleaf Centre UK) began its journey on a cold, damp evening in the spring of 1997, when a few of us with a common interest shoehorned ourselves into a small office at South Bank University to share our ideas on how we might promote the ideas and principles of servant-leadership in the UK. Now, ten years, eleven conferences, many workshops, hundreds of letters, and what seems like a million emails later, we are publishing our first book, and have an opportunity to record our thanks to some of those extraordinary people who have helped us along the way.

Our conferences have been a very important vehicle for introducing servant-leadership in all its settings and applications, and we have been blessed over the years with a number of outstanding presenters from all over the world, more often than not giving their services as a gift to our work. These have included, from the United States, Richard Smith, who facilitated our first two conferences, Jack Lowe, and Bob Ferguson from TDIndustries, Stephanie Alford from Synovus Financial, George SanFacon from the University of Michigan, Julie Beggs, Jeff Miller, Teresa Hogue and Larry Spears. From the southern hemisphere, Diann and Alison Feldman from the Greenleaf Centre Australia and New Zealand have on several occasions travelled half way across the world to come to our conference, and have presented on one occasion. We have had two outstanding contributions from South Africa. In 2003, stepping in at the last moment, Benji Phangela not only introduced us to servant-leadership in South Africa, but led us in dance, too. In 2006, Lance Bloch delivered a memorable all-day workshop based on the South African philosophy of *ubuntu* and the practice of the *umhlanganos*. Jaap Huttenga from the Netherlands has spoken to us on spirituality, Jan Gunnerson from Sweden has shared with us the practice of hostmanship, and Dana Zohar has challenged us to build spiritual capital in our organisations.

Our UK presenters have included Professors Beverley Alimo-Metcalf and Stephen Prosser, Madeline McGill, Debbie Rynda and Jennifer Cramb, Andrew Taylor and Nick Crowder, Jonathan Austin, Andrew Walsh, Sarah Hill, Jane Dawson, Liz Kingsnorth, Bruce Nixon, Jonathan Stanley, Henry Stewart, Judith Leary-Joyce and Lord Brian Griffiths as well as current Greenleaf Board members Charlie Foote, Bob Henry, Ralph Lewis, Stella Smith, Jane Little and Terri McNerney.

There have been changes in our Board over the years, and we would wish to place on record our sincere thanks and appreciation to all those who have given their time and dedication, their insights and commitment to the work we have undertaken. We include here Bruce Lloyd, Sara Miller, Sally Campbell, Jonathan Austin, Gordon Wayne, Susan Dye, Merilyn Parker Armitage and Kate Smith. Special mention should be made of Judith Leary-Joyce, a founder Board member, who served on our Board from 1998 through 2007. Judith has been a wonderful colleague and mentor, and we will miss her wise counsel in the future.

Our particular thanks are due to our good friend and colleague Larry Spears, former President and Chief Executive Officer of the Greenleaf Center in the United States (Greenleaf Center in the USA). Larry has been a staunch ally throughout the first ten years of our centre's existence, always lending support and encouragement when it was most needed, and sometimes prompting the occasional searching question when it was most warranted. We owe him a debt of gratitude that is difficult to articulate and impossible to repay.

Whilst writing this on behalf of the Greenleaf Centre UK Board, I hope I may be forgiven for adding a personal note. I have had the privilege of being deeply involved in all the work we have undertaken over the years, and that has meant many long hours on the computer and quite a considerable time spent away from home. None of this would have been remotely possible without the patience, support and understanding of my wife, Marian, and my daughter, Kirsty. My final, and heartfelt thanks goes to them.

John Noble
For Greenleaf Centre UK Board

Introduction

Welcome to servant-leadership. You may be familiar with the principles, or perhaps the ideas behind servant-leadership may be new to you. Either way, our hope is that this collection of writings from a range of contributors will be an inspiration to you. And that does not mean conversion!

Servant-leadership is not a set of techniques or guidelines to improve productivity or even to make people's working lives better. It is something you do because you believe it is right. Now, there is lots of evidence to suggest that the bottom line is improved and people are happier and more engaged, but again that is not the reason for servant-leadership. You do it because it's the natural thing to do.

This can be illustrated by a story told about Robert Greenleaf (the originator of servant-leadership) and Peter Drucker (one of the world's foremost management gurus) in the 1950s. It happened when both men were conducting a corporate education session. The incident is retold in the *Destiny and the Leader* chapter by Joe Jaworski in *Insights on Leadership*[1], as follows.

"When one of the participants approached with the question, 'What do I do?', Greenleaf responded: 'That comes later. First, what do you want to be?' Drucker recalls that his own 'What do you think will work?' elicited laughter from all three."

Servant-leadership is about who you are as a leader first and foremost. To quote Greenleaf:

"The servant-leader is servant first. It begins with the natural feeling that one wants to serve, to serve first. Then conscious

---

[1] *Insights on Leadership*, ed. Larry C Spears, John Wiley & Sons Inc, 1998

13

choice brings one to aspire to lead. The difference manifests itself in the care taken by the servant-first to make sure that other people's highest priorities are being served."

Sometimes, of course, this is anathema to leaders or managers, especially those who enjoy power and control for its own sake – and too often we confuse service with servility. Servant-leadership is a tough choice, as we will see during the collection of essays in this book. Other people's priority needs are not always what they think they want, and often may appear to conflict with other's needs. Nonetheless, once embarked on, the journey to servant-leadership can be an exhilarating one! The shared experiences in the book are there to help you on your journey – if you want to go along – and if not then we hope they will have provided some food for thought. All the writers with the one exception of James Autry have presented at the Greenleaf Centre UK annual conferences and have much to offer in the way of thoughts, ideas and practical experiences. There are many others we could have asked to write for us with an equal degree of enthusiasm and knowledge – and perhaps we will next time.

John Noble starts with an introduction to the principles and practicalities of servant-leadership, then Ralph Lewis looks at its impact on organisations.

The rest of the chapters are based on the writers' personal experiences of implementing servant-leadership – their successes, their failures, the positive factors and the difficulties. They are an extremely rich and varied source of real and practical applications. Charlie Foote, Bob Henry, Andrew Walsh and Henry Stewart all come from the commercial world. Jane Little and George SanFacon have both had experience of the public sector, one in a large local government and one at a major American University.

Then there are some fascinating stories from those who use servant-leadership in their consultancies. Jaap Huttenga shares with us his reflections on "Yes" and "No" and the introduction of a newly invented 'Yes-culture' in The Netherlands. Jan Gunnarsson is a Swede whose premise is "hostmanship", building a welcoming world. Lance Bloch from South Africa has some profound thoughts about that country's move towards a post-apartheid society and the resolution of the tensions that existed (and still exist). James Autry is one of the best writers and presenters on servant-leadership in the USA (and the world) with practical hands-on experience of running an enormous organisation.

Finally Terri McNerney asks us to reflect on the impact of applying servant-leadership in our lives.

There are many leadership authors and consultants who recognise and honour servant-leadership: Stephen Covey, Peter Senge, Peter Block, Ken Blanchard and Margaret Wheately, to name only a few.

However, this doesn't matter; to return to the beginning, what matters most is you! And, to close with Robert Greenleaf quoting Albert Camus with approval at the end of his essay, *The Servant as Leader*: "Create dangerously."

Contributors

James Autry

James A. Autry is an author, poet, and consultant. Before retiring in 1991, he was president of Meredith Corporation's Magazine Group, a multi million-dollar operation with more than 900 employees. During his 32-year career, Autry served as a daily newspaper reporter, editor of a weekly newspaper, and editor and publisher of various books and magazines. He is an author of many fine works including *Love and Profit, Life and Work, Confessions of an Accidental Businessman*, and *The Servant-Leader*, as well as two collections of poetry, *Nights Under a Tin Roof* and *Life After Mississippi*. He has been a keynote speaker at the Greenleaf Center in the USA's annual international conference on several occasions.

Lance Bloch

Clinical Psychologist Lance Bloch, named Junior Chamber International's 1996 "Outstanding Young Person of the World" for helping reconcile previously warring armies, is recognised as one of the foremost consultants in South Africa and internationally in the areas of Building Workplace Community, Diversity, Leadership Development, Personal Development, Change Management and Transformation, and the originator of the "5th Wave": Culture-Based Behavioural Safety. In addition, both corporates and government, from shop floor to top management, rate him highly for his innovative experiential training and assessment methodology. He has been a keynote speaker at servant-leadership conferences in the USA, UK and South Africa. He can be contacted on 0027-82 4549528 or lbloch@global.co.za.

Charlie Foote

Charlie studied physics at the University of Cambridge. He has spent many years designing and building computer and business systems. He has also been an active entrepreneur and has founded and run his own textile company and, later, one of the top firms of patent attorneys in the UK. He is a long-time supporter of the servant-leader approach to managing businesses. He has given presentations at the annual Greenleaf Centre UK conferences, and is now a member of the Board. He can be contacted on cfoote@btclick.com.

Jan Gunnarsson

Jan Gunnersson is an author and lecturer with more than thirty years of experience from the world of hostmanship. After several years of working directly with guests, he has been engaged in travel destinations, hotels and special attractions in managing, marketing and business development roles, including President of Scandinavian Tourism Inc, USA and Head of Development of the Swedish Travel & Tourism Council. Jan speaks on all aspects of welcoming people, as customers, as co-workers and as partners, and works with clients in all fields of society. Jan is the author of *Hostmanship – The Art of Making People Feel Welcome* and *The Welcoming Leader – The Art of Creating Hostmanship*. He is partner in VÄRDSKAPET AB (Hostmanship Development Group) Stockholm, Sweden. He can be contacted on jan@vardskapet.se.

Olle Blohm

Olle Blohm is an independent writer.

Bob Henry

Bob Henry has over twenty years experience of operating at a senior level in a variety of organisations including main board directorships up to and including CEO. He has a passionate interest in organisational and individual development and has a Masters Degree in Organisational Consulting. He is a director of Dialogix Ltd and focuses primarily on Leadership Development and Coaching with an emphasis on the behavioural aspects of leadership. He has been a supporter of Greenleaf Centre UK since the late 1990s and is a member of the Centre's Board. Bob lives in West Wales on a working farm with his wife Frances. He says running the farm with

Frances is a good way of maintaining a healthy work balance between his organisational work and the farm. He further says that whenever he has any illusions that he is in control a short stint on the farm soon puts that in perspective. He can be contacted on: Dialogix@btinternet.com.

Jaap Huttenga

Jaap was born in Groningen in 1954, in the northern part of The Netherlands, and studied theology at the Free University in Amsterdam. For more than 15 years he was a minister in one of the main protestant churches in the Netherlands. In the year 2000 Jaap started working as a consultant in his own agency, 'Zintern', (a combination of 'zin', a Dutch word which has to do with both joy and meaning, and 'intern' – always start at the inside). Zintern's main issues concern culture of leadership and hierarchy in organisations and the relationship of spirituality and work. In this work the thinking and writings of Robert Greenleaf have inspired him again and again. Together with Ralph Lewis, Jaap developed a workshop, 'Saying Yes', which had its premiere in March this year under the auspices of the Greenleaf Centre UK. Since 2005 Jaap has combined his consultancy with working as a part-time minister. He is married with three children; one of them died four years ago in a traffic accident.

Ralph Lewis

Ralph Lewis co-founded the Greenleaf Centre UK together with John Noble. He was an engineer, systems analyst, volunteer Maths teacher in Uganda and university lecturer before embarking on his present work of leadership consultancy. He has written many articles and several books focusing on Jung and organisations, and is a keen listener to world music. He is married to Arabella with a son David and daughter Ruth and lives in the beautiful Stroud valleys. He can be contacted on ralph.lewis@virgin.net.

Jane Little

Jane Little started by working in her local library on Saturdays in the year when *Sgt. Pepper's Lonely Hearts Club Band* was released. She went on to build a traditional career in public libraries, working for several councils in London and roundabout. Her eyes were then opened to new ways of working (including servant-leadership) and, through a series of secondments and experiments, she created a role for herself leading organisational change in a major London borough. She's still there and expects to carry on, deepening the conversations, until servant-leadership is established, or she finds another place to talk about it.

Terri McNerney
Terri McNerney is a trustee of the Greenleaf Centre UK and set up Inspire in 1999, as a small specialist consultancy. As coach and facilitator, Terri specialises in developing and aligning leadership teams, and supporting organisations through change and post-merger integration. Terri has more than twenty years experience with Global 500 companies and holds an MSc in Organisational Consulting from Ashridge School of Management. She is based in London. See www.inspirethebest.com.

John Noble
John Noble worked in both the scientific and financial Civil Service before being appointed Personnel Manager for the central work of London (later Britain) Yearly Meeting of the Religious Society of Friends (Quakers), with overall responsibility for the personnel matters for both their UK and two-thirds world work. He played a leading role in early 1997 in setting up the Greenleaf UK and, since leaving his post with Quakers in 2002, John has devoted the greater part of his time, as voluntary Administrator and Director of the Centre, to developing and extending its work. John has led and contributed to a large number of conferences, workshops and seminars on servant-leadership principles and practice with groups of consultants, leaders, managers and wider staff groups throughout the UK and in Australia, Europe, South Africa, and the United States. He can be contacted on jnoble@greenleaf.netkonect.co.uk.

George SanFacon
George SanFacon served as Director of Housing Facilities at the

University of Michigan from 1983 to 2004. During his time there, he successfully implemented a "council of equals" governance framework based on Robert K Greenleaf's *primus inter pares* model described in "The Institution as Servant". George describes the framework and how it works in two publications: *The Council Handbook* and *Awake at Work*, both of which are available at the University of Michigan's website. Since leaving the University, George has been living "below the radar" as a caretaker at a small retreat centre in the lakes region of beautiful south-eastern Michigan. In his spare time, George continues to study and write about leadership and organisational governance. He is presently revising and expanding *Awake at Work*, and co-authoring a monograph on "Full Spectrum Servant-leadership" with Larry Spears, President Emeritus of the Greenleaf Center in the USA.

Henry Stewart
Henry Stewart is founder and Chief Executive of Happy, a training company based in central London. His company has been rated the best in the UK for customer service, the best for work-life balance, the 2nd best workplace and the best small company in terms of impact on society. Prior to Happy Computers, Henry was involved in setting up a radical tabloid Sunday newspaper called News on Sunday. He describes much of what he has achieved at Happy as stemming from what he learned about what not to do at News on Sunday. He left determined not to work for others again, and to find out what did make a company both principled and effective, and a great place to work. A major passion is how to make learning enjoyable and relevant to people of all ages. He is Chair of Governors of his local comprehensive, and Chair of the charity Antidote, which works to help schools become emotionally literate, and campaigns to promote state education and oppose selection. Henry is also active in politics, managing the web site for Jews for Justice and Human Right (JFJHR) and Independent Jewish Voices, of which he is a founding member. Other interests include cycling and re-evaluation counselling, which he practises and teaches.

Andrew Walsh

Andrew is obsessed with the premise that successful business strategy can only be achieved if the people, culture and structure are completely congruent with it. He has pursued this goal over the last 25 years with roles in the commercial, public and voluntary sectors. For the last six years he has led the people function at the Pensions Trust, an occupational pensions business for charities and the not-for-profit sector. Prior to that, he was Airport Personnel Manager at Leeds Bradford Airport. When not working to develop culture, Andrew plays piano with a jazz group and rides classic British motorcycles. He lives with his wife, Vibeke, and daughter, Fenella, in Harrogate, North Yorkshire.

The Principles of
Servant-Leadership

1

Principles and Practicalities

John Noble

"Write people's virtues on a tablet of stone and their faults on the sands of the seashore."

WC Bradley

Introduction

Servant-leadership is in many ways an old idea but, in expressing it in the way he did in the context of the late 20th century business world, Robert Greenleaf presents us with something of a new paradigm, and one which in many ways perhaps still runs contrary to prevailing ideas of exercising power and managing people.

Who was Robert Greenleaf?

Robert Greenleaf was an American Quaker, from Terre Haute, Indiana. In his final year at college one of his professors offered the thought that institutions were becoming increasingly large and influential and would continue to grow in influence without necessarily serving their constituents well. His view was that such institutions – *multinationals*, although the word was not known at the time – seldom changed from the outside, so if the students wanted to have an influence on future events, they should consider joining one of those larger institutions and encourage change from within. At that time the largest company in America was AT&T, and Greenleaf joined, first as a posthole digger and lineman, and eventually as Head of Management Research. In later years, he turned down promotions so that he could stay where he felt he could be most useful.

After taking retirement at 60, Greenleaf launched on a second career as a consultant, undertaking long-term contracts with a small number of clients, among them universities. In order to help with the communication between the faculty, the administration and the students he decided to find out what the students were reading, what was informing their thinking. He discovered that they were reading Hermann Hess, with *Journey to the East* the most popular of his works at the time.

In *Servant-Leadership – A Journey into the Nature of Legitimate Power and Greatness*[2], Greenleaf describes *Journey to the East* as follows.

> *"In this story we see a band of men on a mythical journey, probably Hesse's own journey. The central figure of the story is Leo, who accompanies the party as the servant who does their menial chores, but who also sustains them with his spirit and his song. He is a person of extraordinary presence. All goes well until Leo disappears. Then the group falls into disarray and the journey is abandoned. They cannot make it without the servant Leo. The narrator, one of the party, after some years of wandering finds Leo and is taken into the Order that had sponsored the journey. There he discovers that Leo, whom he had known first as servant, was in fact the titular head of the Order, its guiding spirit, a great and noble leader."*

The point of the story is that we see Leo, who was really the group's leader and inspiration, initially in the role of servant. From this Greenleaf deduced that great leaders must first serve others, and that

---

[2] Robert K. Greenleaf, *Servant Leadership – A Journey into the Nature of Legitimate Power and Greatness*, Paulist Press, 2002

this plain fact is central to that greatness. In other words, authentic leadership emerges from those whose principal motivation is an aspiration to help and develop others.

The main emphases of servant-leadership are:

- increased service to others
- a holistic approach to work
- the building of a sense of community in the workplace
- a wider sharing of power in decision-making.

All in all, it is a powerful principle that promotes organisational earning because it offers a way to engage the knowledge and wisdom of *all* employees, not just those at the top. And that is why it is so important in change.

There are, unquestionably, some stops in the mind when one uses the phrase 'servant-leadership'. It is a phrase that makes some people uncomfortable. 'Service' is often associated with work that is either undignified or unworthy. In some people's minds service is seen as submissive or servile. But let's look at what we mean by service. I think it's summed up well by George SanFacon formerly of the University of Michigan in his book, *Awake at Work*[3], when when he says:

"Service is not simply a New Age product and workplace phenomenon, but an activity and function that is woven throughout the fabric of human community, the essence of which is interaction and interdependence. As community members, we are called to support one another informally in countless ways – through common courtesies, thoughtful gestures and the simplest moments of human affirmation."

Greenleaf also offers us the rationale that servant-leadership is a pathway to a better, more caring society:

"If a better society is to be built, one that is more just and more loving, one that provides greater creative opportunity for

---

[3] George SanFacon, *Awake at Work,* 2002 & 2004 and Ram Dass and Paul Gorman, *How Can I Help?*, Alfred A. Knop, 1987

its people, then the most open course is to raise both the capacity to serve and the very performance as servant of existing major institutions by new regenerative forces operating within them."[4]

Who is the servant-leader?

Robert Greenleaf himself gave us what many still consider the best definition of the servant-leader, as follows:

"The servant-leader is servant first. It begins with the natural feeling that one wants to serve, to serve first. Then conscious choice brings one to aspire to lead. The difference manifests itself in the care taken by the servant-first to make sure that other people's highest priorities are being served. The best test, and difficult to administer, is: Do those served grow as persons? Do they, while being served, become healthier, wiser, freer, more autonomous, more likely themselves to become servants? And what is the effect on the least privileged in society; will they benefit or, at least, not be further deprived?"[5]

It is important to note that servant-leadership applies to both designated and situational leaders; it does not depend on positional authority.

Characteristics of servant-leadership

My friend and colleague, Larry Spears, has spent many years studying the writings of Robert Greenleaf and has gleaned from these a list of ten characteristics of servant-leaders. He describes them as follows:

---

[4] Robert K Greenleaf, *Servant Leadership – A Journey into the Nature of Legitimate Power and Greatness*, Paulist Press, 2002
[5] ibid

Listening

Leaders have traditionally been valued for their communication and decision-making skills. While these are also important skills for the servant-leader, they need to be reinforced by a deep commitment to listen intently to others. The servant-leader seeks to identify the will of the group and helps clarify that will. Listening, coupled with regular periods of reflection, is essential to the growth of the servant-leader.

Empathy

The servant-leader strives to understand and empathise with others.

People need to be accepted and recognised for their special and unique spirits. One assumes the good intentions of co-workers and does not reject them as people, even while refusing to accept their behaviour or performance.

Healing

Learning to heal is a powerful force for transformation and integration.

One of the great strengths of servant-leadership is the potential for healing one's self and others. Many people have broken spirits and have suffered from a variety of emotional hurts. Although this is a part of being human, servant-leaders recognise that they have an opportunity to help make whole those with whom they come in contact.

Awareness

General awareness, and especially self-awareness, strengthens the servant-leader. Awareness also aids one in understanding issues involving ethics and values. It lends itself to being able to view most situations from a more integrated, holistic position.

Persuasion

The servant-leader seeks to convince others, rather than using positional authority in making decisions within an organisation. The servant-leader seeks to convince others, rather than coerce compliance. This particular element offers one of the clearest distinctions between the traditional authoritarian model and that of servant-leadership.

Conceptualisation

Servant-leaders seek to nurture their abilities to dream great dreams.

The ability to look at a problem (or organisation) from a conceptualising perspective means that one must think beyond day-to-day realities. The traditional manager is consumed by the need to achieve short-term operational goals. The manager who wishes also to be a servant-leader must stretch his or her thinking to encompass broader-based, conceptual thinking.

Foresight

The ability to foresee the likely outcome of a situation is hard to define, but easy to identify. Foresight is a characteristic that enables the servant-leader to understand the lessons from the past, the realities of the present, and the likely consequence of a decision for the future.

It is also deeply rooted within the intuitive mind. As such, one can conjecture that foresight is the one servant-leader characteristic with which one may be born. All other characteristics can be consciously developed.

Stewardship

Peter Block (1993) has defined stewardship as holding something in trust for another. Servant-leadership, like stewardship, assumes first and foremost a commitment to serving the needs of others.

It also emphasises the use of openness and persuasion rather than control.

Commitment to the growth of people

Servant-leaders believe that people have an intrinsic value beyond their tangible contributions as workers. As such, the servant-leader is deeply committed to the growth of each and every individual within his or her institution. The servant-leader recognises the tremendous responsibility to do everything within his or her power to nurture the personal, professional and spiritual growth of employees.

Building community

The servant-leader senses that much has been lost in recent human history as a result of the shift from local communities to large institutions as the primary shaper of human lives. This awareness causes the servant-leader to seek to identify some means for building community among those who work within a given institution. Servant-leadership suggests that true community can be created among those who work in business and other institutions. Greenleaf said, all that is needed to rebuild community as a viable life form for large numbers of people is for enough servant-leaders to show the way, not by mass movements, but by each servant-leader demonstrating his or her own unlimited liability for a quite specific community-related group.

(Based on the writing of Larry C Spears)

I would certainly not argue that these characteristics are exclusive to those practicing servant-leadership, and would suggest that two further characteristics, those of modesty and humility would readily find a place in the servant-leader's make up.

In some ways the characteristics that Larry Spears gleaned from Greenleaf's work were also summed up in what Hyler Bracey *et al* in *Managing from the Heart*[6] call the "five unspoken employee requests":

- Even if you disagree with me, don't make me wrong.
- Hear and understand me.
- Tell me the truth with compassion.
- Remember to look for my loving intentions.
- Acknowledge the greatness within me.

---

[6] Hyler Bracey, Jack Rosenblum, Aubrey Sanford & Roy Trueblood, *Managing from the Heart*, Dell Publishing 1990

Trust

"My father imposed upon me the greatest discipline: he trusted me."

Robert Galvin former CEO of Motorola

A good and wise friend of mine once shared the thought that references should always be written in double spacing, so that the recipient could read between the lines! I have often thought that the list of servant-leadership characteristics should be similarly written out, with the word "trust" clearly positioned in the space between each one. Think back for a moment about those people in your life whom you would regard as authentic leaders, people who meant a great deal to you, people you would willingly follow, and why. I have asked workshop audiences all over the world precisely this question, and while I have received a large number of different responses, inevitably one of those will be that the person in question "trusted me".

And ask yourself, in the whole of your working life how many people can you recall who didn't want to do their best? Unless you are very unusual or very unlucky you will come up with a very small number. And yet by and large our personnel policies seem designed for the small minority – the ones who, for whatever reason, do not want to do their best, who cannot be trusted. To work on the basis that people by and large cannot be trusted is deeply impractical; it has no effect on the very ones who are not trustworthy, and sends a deeply negative message to those who are.

Ask yourself another question: How do you work best? When someone tells you exactly what to do, how to do it and then micromanages every step of the way? Or rather when you agree what is needed, are set tight targets but are then trusted to carry it out using all your initiative, experience, flair and imagination? You know what the answer is – and it's the same answer for pretty well everyone you can think of. We all know that we work well on trust, and I firmly believe that in our daily lives, whether it is in our personal or our working relationships, trust is the only logical option. It is at the very heart of servant-leadership and is its most fundamental principle.

32

The relevance of servant-leadership for today

"I personally experience that sense of right-timeliness to this body of work called servant-leadership. I feel that for more and more of us we need to realise that it will take even more courage to move it forward, but that the necessity to move it forward is clear."[7]

Servant-leadership is not simply some sort of theoretical idea. It has to be clearly seen in our actions; what we do every day. So how do we go about becoming a servant-leader?

A few years ago, Larry Spears and I met and interviewed James Autry, the former President of the magazine group for the Meredith Corporation, and currently a major business consultant, writer, speaker, and poet. In the course of that meeting he offered us five attributes, five ways of being that will move us towards a more meaningful expression of servant-leadership in every setting. He described them briefly as follows:

- **Be Authentic** – be who you are, bringing all your values to every situation.

- **Be Vulnerable** – be honest with your feelings in the context of your work

- **Be Accepting** – be prepared to hear those views and ideas you may not like. Strive to create the win/win solution where there are no losers.

- **Be Present** – live in the moment, practise "nowness".

- **Be Useful** – be a resource for those around you, a servant.

Jim also gave us three reasons for what he saw as a growth in the interest in servant-leadership and its relevance for today:

---

[7] Margaret Wheatley with John Noble and Larry C Spears, 'The Servant Leader: From Hero to Host', included in *Practicing Servant Leadership: Succeeding Through Trust, Bravery and Forgiveness*, Jossey-Bass, 2004

1. **The increasing number, and influence, of women in the workplace**

   There are two factors in this; the impact of motherhood, and the need to balance those demands against work-place demands, and the fact that women tend to socialise by affiliation and men by separation. These are to some extent simplifications but the differences certainly seem to be having an influence on workplace culture.

2. **Unemployment**

   This has been much lower than in the past twenty-five years and, increasingly, people tend to look for more flexibility and openness to new ideas and different thinking in their prospective employer.

And, finally–

3. **The old ways simply were not working!**

Where servant-leadership is working

I am often asked to provide demonstrable examples of servant-leadership working successfully in organisations, and this can most readily be done by simply referring any enquirer to the list of companies that have regularly featured in the *Fortune Magazine* assessment of the *100 Best Companies to Work for in America*. Companies such as **TDIndustries**, a Dallas based mechanical engineering and servicing company, **Synovus Financial**, a diversified financial services holding company with more than $24 billion in assets based in Columbus, Georgia, and **Southwest Airlines**, now widely regarded as the most successful airline in the world, offer clear evidence, both in terms of employee satisfaction and financial success, of the beneficial effects of servant-leadership.

However, I have become increasingly disinclined to respond to requests to provide working examples to promote servant-leadership because I believe that, to a great extent, this misses the point. It has to be remembered that servant-leadership is not an "off the peg", "one size fits all" set of principles.

It works in the examples given above because in some cases the founders, and certainly the current leadership *truly believe* that the principles of servant-leadership provide the right way to deal with the issues of exercising power and managing people. Appropriate structures, policies and governance framework come afterwards, of course, but the belief has to be there – and genuinely so – first.

I recall being at a convention in Columbus, Georgia some eight years ago, when someone in the audience asked the panel composed largely of CEOs of servant-leadership companies, how to go about establishing servant-leadership in a new company he was about to set up. The response from the panel was, simply, "You have the intention." Then the rider: "If you adopt servant-leadership because you believe it will make you a profit, it will fail. If you adopt servant-leadership because you believe it is the right thing to do, you will be profitable."

It is important to dismiss the notion that perhaps servant-leadership is some sort of new-age gimmicky notion – some form of 'soft management'.

Servant-leaders know that H. L. Mencken was right when he said, "There is always an easy solution to every human problem – neat, plausible, and wrong." Servant-leadership is not figuratively lying around eating jam donuts and listening to Eddie Fisher records. It's about agreeing high standards and then creating a place of safety and support where people are then trusted to do their best work. It's also about getting rid of ego, building a community in the workplace, and realising that the only power you have comes from the people you lead. As Robert Greenleaf's biographer, Don Frick said in *Robert K Greenleaf: A Life of Servant-leadership:*

> *"If you are weary of management and leadership 'tips and techniques', if you are prepared to go deeper to achieve higher distinction, consider the ideas and practices of servant-leadership. Be prepared for the ride of your life, though. Robert Greenleaf's own experience proved that this is not a soft or easy journey."[8]*

---

[8] Don M. Frick, *Robert K Greenleaf: A Life of Servant Leadership*, Berrett-Koehler, 2004

Establishing servant-leadership as the governance principle in an organisation or setting where previously the old ways prevailed is a daunting prospect. I am reminded of the story of the American tourist who finds himself entirely lost in a remote area of Scotland. Spotting a local fellow out walking his dog, he pulls his car to the side of the road and asks for directions to Edinburgh. "Edinburgh? says the local, shaking his head, " Och, I wouldnae start from here!" Many of us know how that feels. But we can only start where we are, and often it can seem that stretching before us is a long and hazardous road. I clearly recall being on that path myself some years ago and drawing comfort from the words of the American Quaker, Rufus Jones 1863–1948, who said, "I pin my hopes to quiet processes and small circles, in which vital and transforming events take place." It would, of course, be wonderful if everyone adopted the principles of servant-leadership immediately; it is far more likely that the change will come gradually, one small step at a time.

While many of us believe that servant-leadership is a logical, sensible and morally apposite way of running any organisation – Stephen Covey has called it "a natural law" – the fact remains that few organisations claim to operate by reference to its principles, and it is still regarded, admittedly by those of a less than sympathetic frame of mind as soft, vague, or even counter-cultural. The implication in all of this is that somehow servant-leadership is easy, but any such notion will be discounted in even the briefest of journeys through the pages of this book.

At its core, servant-leadership is about values and, unlike the Hollywood mogul quoted in a later chapter, there are no spares to fall back on if the going gets difficult. It is not a case of "well things are rough so we'll slip back into the old ways until it picks up, and then we can be servant-leaders again." It's a daft notion in any event. Indeed, as Jim Autry has pointed out in his book, *The Servant-Leader*, "servant-leadership is not only good-time leadership. Its value to you and your people has even more meaning and impact during the times when people are worried and struggling."[9] The

---

[9] James Autry, *The Servant Leader*, Prima Publishing, 2001

servant-leader also recognises what David Whyte means when he says: "The consummation of work lies not only in what we have done, but who we have become while accomplishing the task."[10]

Servant-leadership can be thought of as both an old idea and a contemporary concept. Where we are at the moment is on a path that stretches back into a known past and on into an uncertain future, and as such the question of legacy becomes of even greater significance. Legacy is widely defined as things handed *down* to a successor. I have always strongly held the view that one of the leader's principal duties is always to be looking to prepare her or his successor, or at the very least prepare the ground for that successor in the hope, belief and expectation that the work, whatever it may be, will be done better in the future.

And what of that future? How can we servant-leaders create the time, the space and the opportunity to make it possible for the next generation of leaders to begin to develop their vision now? So much is spoken and written about *change* as if it were a noun and not a verb, and those who are so often at the heart of it all will either not be around when the implications come to full fruition, or will likely be unable to bring any truly visionary thinking along the way. Organisations, particularly perhaps those in the not-for-profit sector, tend to remain stuck. There must surely be a connection between our (thus far) unwillingness to work with the next generation's vision and the inescapable fact that to a great extent the majority of our current leaders have very much the same attitudes as the previous generation and the one before that.

What can we say and do as servant-leaders to help break the cycle and bring forward the time when the leadership roles can be carried by younger people, thus bringing fresh insights and longer-term fundamental change to our organisations? How can we begin to develop the role of the older generation as the coaches, mentors and servants to the process? It is a challenge for the servant-leader in all of us.

---

[10] David Whyte, *The Heart Aroused (revised edition)*, Articulate Press, 2007

2

Serving Organisations

Ralph Lewis

"The business exists to provide meaningful work for the person as it exists to provide a product or service to the customer."

Robert Greenleaf

Introduction

Robert Greenleaf entered AT&T, then the biggest public company in the world after his graduation. He joined in the mid 1920s as a result of a talk from one of his professors. The statement from his professor was along these lines:

"There is a new problem in our country. We are becoming a nation that is dominated by large institutions – churches, businesses, governments, labour unions, universities – and these big institutions are not serving us well. I hope all of you will be concerned about this. Now you can do as I do, stand outside and criticise, bring pressure if you can, write and argue about it. All of this may do some good. But nothing of substance will happen unless there are people inside these institutions who are able (and want) to lead them into better performance for the public good. Some of you ought to make careers inside these big institutions and become a force for good – from the inside."[11]

---

[11] Robert K. Greenleaf, *Servant Leadership,* Paulist Press, 1977

Many years on these words are just as applicable – perhaps even more so in the light of the corporate scandals that have soured public confidence in leaders of all institutions – political, social and business.

This chapter will look at the purpose and structure underlying organisations and a way of analysing what needs to happen for them to be successful. We will then look at what servant-leadership can offer us in any quest to improve them. There are several examples of servant-leadership organisations that are both highly successful in business terms and yet stay true to the core principles of servant-leadership. And finally, what can we do to become a "force for good – from the inside" so that we can help organisations become serving organisations?

Underpinning all of this is a belief that servant-leadership can manifest itself in many forms. Balance and diversity are essential in any servant-leadership organisation and the true servant-leader recognises that in serving others he or she must come from a position of understanding their own preferences whilst recognising other's differences.

So why do organisations exist?

Asking this question of business leaders usually provokes a number of passionate and deeply held beliefs – and an inability to accept others' points of view. Often the discussion becomes polarised with those on one side insisting that organisations exist purely for the benefit of the shareholders and are there solely to make money for them – and those who have a variety of other thoughts – like serving the customer or looking after employees. (Although there is often a difference between theory and practice with business leaders – I remember a senior manager insisting that his organisation, which was making a loss, should be closed down and the money invested in a bank to provide a better return to shareholders. The employees didn't matter, he insisted. Six weeks later his company was taken over and one of his first actions was to join a union so that his job would be protected!)

And they are all right, of course! Organisations are multi-purpose, complex structures that exist for a variety of purposes – and the first step in service is to recognise this. The second step is to acknowledge that our own view of what organisations should be is coloured by our own personalities. Research has shown that different personality types focus on different aspects and purposes of organisations.[12]

To be a true servant-leader is to understand your own biases with regard to institutions and to develop a capacity for balance and wholeness in the service of others. This applies to individuals and to organisations, whatever their focus. They must rise above their prejudices and biases and lead in a whole and embracing way – accepting and valuing many diverse viewpoints. These differences can be grouped into four key areas – the four functions of organisations.

The simplest definition of an organisation is "a group of people with common goals". It does not matter whether the organisation is industrial or social, very small or immensely large, simple or complex, this definition applies. There may be disagreement (and often is) over the common goals, but essentially the definition implies that people are co-operating in some fashion to achieve something they have agreed on. When people work together there are essential things they need to do; talking to each other for example or carrying out specific tasks. Researchers looking at groups working as teams defined four key functions and they apply equally to organisations. These are:

1. Dealing with those outside the organisation – clients, shareholders, governments, etc. – anyone involved with the organisation.
2. Dealing with the world outside the organisation (getting supplies – materials, money, etc., and selling finished products).
3. Doing things to produce things (be it goods or services).
4. Keeping those working within the organisation happy and satisfied so they stay and work.

---

[12] Mitroff, I.I., Kilman, R.H., 'Stories Managers Tell: A New Tool for Organisational Problem-Solving', *Management Review 64(7)*, 1975

These functions can be plotted as follows:

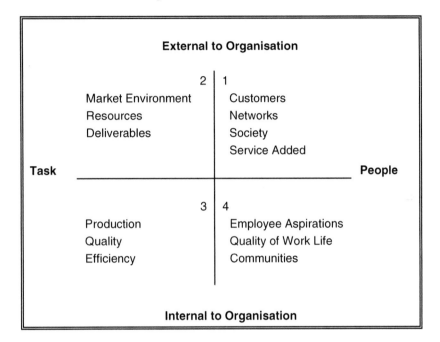

Figure 1. The Four Functions of Organisation

If an organisation fails in any of these areas it will fail totally! If an organisation does not look after its employees well enough they will leave as soon as they can and the organisation will collapse. If people are hopeless at doing what they are supposed to do (making things, or providing a service), customers will go elsewhere (at least in non-monopoly situations). This applies as much to not-for-profit institutions, although it may take longer for the poor performance to become visible on the two external functions. If a group of people cannot get resources from the market place, or interact with their physical or economic environment adequately, they will be unable to continue. If they break society's laws or treat clients badly, again they will not be allowed to survive. The United States, for example, has an admirable record in regulating this area with regard to consumer rights. All these aspects are more evident in an open society but even in a closed environment, although people may be bound to continue working for a particular group, they will leave psychologically and work will not be done effectively or with heart.

The framework can be used further. All organisations need to ensure that they are functioning adequately in each of the above areas, but they can also be classified in terms of their primary focus within one of the functions/quadrants. Producers of fast-moving consumer goods, for example, will generally be market-driven. Their purpose is to compete and grow – to gain market share. They are in the External-Task quadrant. Their underlying values are about being biggest and best. The two leading cola producers (Coca-Cola and Pepsi-Cola) are obvious examples. It is sometimes difficult to imagine where either of these two companies would be without the other to compete with. Their rationale lies in defeating competitors – the "enemy". When viewed in this way the constant mergers and takeovers that occur in business can be understood as a need for growth and game-playing rather than any real attempt to add economic value. (Most mergers or takeovers destroy economic value.)

Production-led organisations (Internal-Task) have as their prime purpose manufacture of products or delivery of service in terms of quality and efficiency. Their values are competency and stability. The automobile industry, for example, has to focus on manufacture of cars or other means of transport efficiently with emphasis on task specialisation, economies of scale and effective use of assets. Of course, marketing functions need to be carried out and products tailored to what clients want to buy, but the prime purpose of the car industry is to make affordable quality cars. The Japanese car industry got all these areas right well before Western firms did.

Employee-focused organisations (Internal-People) are almost non-existent in the business world. These organisations exist for the benefit of their members. Examples of these in the non-business world are many such as the Scout Movement, Alcoholics Anonymous, sports clubs and, in some cases, political parties. The family is also an example of this type of organisation; its common goal is the support and nourishment of the members of the family. However, pursuing this theme, the family, as an organisation, also needs to fulfil the other functions if it is to be viable: resources need to be brought into the organisation such as food, clothing, etc.; specific tasks such as cooking, washing, house maintenance need to be carried out; and the family needs to coexist with non-members such as neighbours.

The last area of organisational functioning is that of the service organisation – the External-People quadrant. This has as its goal the delivery of a service to others – clients, customers, whatever. Key examples would be educational, health and religious organisations where the focus is, or at least should be, helping others. Again, to go back to the four functions, institutions need to be cost-effective in the way they perform tasks, they need to gain resources to carry out services effectively, and they also need to value their members and reward them appropriately for helping to deliver the organisation's service. But all these aspects are secondary to the prime goal of service. Thus if we find a service organisation competing against "rivals", or trying to raise money to enable it to be bigger than other institutions, or rewarding some of its members with inappropriately large salaries, then it is quite legitimate to question these activities. If an organisation does this it will have lost sight of its purpose. Equally inappropriate would be these organisations focusing on their survival when they are no longer needed by their clients.

One other over-riding aspect needs to be added – the country that the organisation is in. Different countries focus on different aspects of organisations. One key dimension seems to be the "head-heart" dimension or "principles-relationships". The USA is towards the head or task end of the continuum and it shares this orientation with much of the Anglo-Saxon world – Canada, Germany and the UK, for example. Countries at the "heart" or "people" end would be much of Latin-America, Japan and France, for example.[13]

This distinction is of key importance to the way that people

---

[13] Trompenaars, F., *Riding the Waves of Culture*, Economist Books, 1993

conduct themselves in everyday life. In a task oriented society the focus is on objectivity, equality and getting the task done. There often is less structure around people interactions and less status (which sometimes goes with less respect for leaders, so less status can also be negative). The principles of law come first before loyalty to friends and family. This gives a society in which the focus is on what you do rather than who you are but the social support networks that exist in a people oriented society are often lacking. In a "heart" society, respect for others, if they are in particular groupings, and loyalty to those groupings, come first rather than emphasis on getting the task done. This can lead to inefficiency and favouring of one dominant group over the other but the advantages are a sense of community and belonging.

So the "rules" prevailing within different societies will have a profound impact upon the way in which relationships are governed, and the way institutions function and provide service. The culture will further orientate organisations and individuals towards the head or heart poles and towards the way work is viewed.

Individuals and institutions

Organisation culture derives from the values and assumptions of those in power in those organisations – the leaders – and there is a clear consistent link between individual personality and organisation culture. The main findings linking these areas were researched by Kilmann and Mitroff.[14] When you look at business leaders in the USA and the UK they emphasise tasks and growth, not people. Of course, these are simplifications but they enable some general conclusions to be drawn. It would be expected that because of the focus on task in industrial and commercial organisations, the people side, the areas that have the least individuals of those types, may well be neglected. This takes us back to Robert Greenleaf's quote at the beginning and explains why his clear insights are so often neglected by business leaders – their goals are to do with economics and task

---

[14] Mitroff, I.I., Kilman, R.H., ibid

attainment rather than individual meaning and growth. However, conversely, within institutions where the focus is on service the neglected areas would be efficiency and task achievement. But herein lies the dilemma – if there is not a minimum level of standards in the task area the institution will not be able to provide a worthwhile service because it will be inefficient and neglect quality. Conversely, too much emphasis on production and task will take away the human quality of interaction. For example hospitals are places where technical knowledge and expertise is essential but what patients require most is to be treated as human beings, to have their feelings acknowledged and dealt with sympathetically. Thus we are back to balance and wholeness – the head/heart, task/person equilibrium.

Servant-leadership and institutions

An effective institution must strike the right balance between task and person orientation. The role of the leader is absolutely critical in this, given that organisations are very much made in their image. So, if an institution is to provide a service that balances task and people aspects, then the leader must be appreciative of this need for balance themselves. The difficulty, of course, is learning how to achieve the balance – how to get tasks done by maintaining respect for people. There have been leaders in history who have combined task efficiency with human warmth – Napoleon, for example, being one of these – but they have been few and far between.[15]

To return to Robert Greenleaf:

"Personally, I would prefer to pay a higher price if thereby the institution could become substantially more serving to all who are touched by its actions.

Having said all this I recognise the problem of so much of business not serving well. But the core of the problem, as I see it, is not in business institutions; rather it is in the attitudes,

---

[15] Dixon, N., *On the Psychology of Military Incompetence*, Futura, 1976

*concepts and expectations regarding business held by the rest of society. People in churches, universities, government and social agencies **do not love** business institutions. As a consequence, many inside businesses do not love them either. Businesses, despite their crassness, occasional corruption, and unloviness, **must be loved** if they are to serve us better. They are much too large a presence in the lives of us all to have them in our midst and **not** serve us better.*

*But how, one may ask, can one love this abstraction called the corporation? One doesn't! One loves **only the people** who are gathered to render the service for which the corporation is enfranchised. **The people are the institution!**"[16]*

To reiterate, this is not an easy path. Servant-leadership is not a soft option – peace and love don't automatically produce quality performance. The focus on people is within the context of service – ensuring that, as Greenleaf said, the highest priority *needs* of people are met. This includes products and services that work, attention to detail, transport that runs on time, etc. In other words the balance of hitting "hard" financial and other business targets with respect and care for people.

Serving organisations

There are a few organisations that have espoused servant-leadership deliberately as part of their corporate philosophy. (There are probably many others that practise a form of servant-leadership without calling it such.) These organisations combine business success with investment in people and relationships and a strong ethical base. They serve as inspiration to us all.

The servant-leadership organisations in the USA include Southwest Airlines, TDIndustries, Starbucks Coffee, The Carrollton Police Service in Texas, Synovus Financial Corporation, Men's Warehouse and ServiceMaster. In the UK there are companies that

---

[16] Robert K. Greenleaf, ibid

operate along the principles of servant-leadership without necessarily claiming to be servant-leadership organisations. Happy, for example, a computer training company, has a core principle of its leadership being there to support the people in it and to put them first. These are all organisations that put people at the core of their business – and as a result are extremely successful in their business worlds.

Two specific examples are Southwest Airlines and TDIndustries. Both are in businesses which are extremely tough commercially and both are very successful financially. They combine great business expertise with profound respect for people and explicity operate using servant-leadership as part of their driving principles. As has been said before servant-leadership is not a soft option! It requires a great deal of courage, honesty and determination.

Southwest Airlines

Southwest Airlines is a low-fare airline based in Dallas, Texas. Its business performance is truly amazing for an airline. It is the largest airline in the USA by number of passengers carried domestically for any one year and the second largest airline in the world by number of passengers carried. Southwest Airlines is one of the world's most profitable airlines and in January 2007, made a profit for the 34th consecutive year. The number of complaints per passenger is the lowest in the USA and it has won many awards for business ethics and also for being top of Fortune magazine's annual survey of a great place to work.

In the weeks following 9/11 Southwest Airlines, unlike its competitors, refused to lay off employees although this was costing it $1 million per day. A year later US Airways had lost 95.7% of its stock value, Southwest was the least affected with a loss of only 16.6%. Focusing on building a service culture which includes all people works! Southwest has always had a consistent emphasis on valuing its people. The corporate culture is both innovative and "love-based" with emphasis on fun and enjoyment. It is also known for its financial acumen – witness the business results. Some of this comes from its financial management – hedging fuel prices for example. Southwest CEO Gary Kelly has been ranked as one of America's top

CEO's and was ranked best CEO in the airline sector in 2006.
Southwest's mission statement reads as follows:

> *"Southwest Airlines is dedicated to the highest quality of
> Customer Service delivered with a sense of warmth,
> friendliness, individual pride, and Company Spirit.*
>
> *We are committed to provide our Employees a stable work
> environment with equal opportunity for learning and personal
> growth. Creativity and innovation are encouraged for
> improving the effectiveness of Southwest Airlines. Above all,
> Employees will be provided with the same concern, respect,
> and caring attitude within the Organisation that they are
> expected to share externally with every Southwest Customer.*
>
> *Southwest Airlines top management team has several core
> values that it relies on to lead the organisation. One central
> value is **a belief in people**. Southwest is known to look for the
> "right kind of people" in its hiring processes. A second core
> value is simplicity of Southwest's product and its delivery
> system. A third core value is building lasting relationships
> with employees and customers. The fourth core value is the
> importance of investment. Southwest's investment is not just in
> machines or capital but also in people. It invests time and
> effort in building relationships within Southwest and with
> external parties such as suppliers and air traffic controllers. It
> has more operations agents than other airlines and more
> supervisors, enabling them to coach and work with front-line
> employees. The management team also invests in
> communicating with one another, enabling it to develop
> shared goals, shared knowledge and respect and co-
> ordination at the top, which transfers all through the
> organisation. The willingness to invest in relationships may
> well be the core value that sets Southwest Airlines apart."*[17]

---

[17] See also Southwest Airlines' blog, 'Nuts', at www.blogsouthwest.com

TDIndustries

TDIndustries was No. 2 in the *100 Best Companies to work for in America* in 1999, and has been consistently in the top ten. It has 1500 employees. TDIndustries is a mechanical engineering and servicing company and is explicit about its focus on applying the servant-leadership model. Its mission statement, as published on its website, reads:

> *"TDIndustries customers and employees work together in a partnership of the spirit to fulfill its mission.*
>
> *We are committed to providing* **outstanding career opportunities** *by exceeding our customers' expectations through continuous aggressive improvement."*

TDIndustries is committed to the accomplishment of this mission over the long term. They do not believe in seizing short-term benefits to the detriment of their long term mission. They believe in continuous, intense "people-development" efforts, including substantial training budgets. They believe in investing in tools, equipment and facilities that enable them to better accomplish their mission.

Bob Ferguson, Managing Director of TDIndustries Inc, says: "In his book, *The Servant as Leader*, Robert Greenleaf successfully expressed our views of how people can and should work together to grow our company. If our organisation is to live up to its basic values and mission, a key ingredient will be the leadership provided by a very large number of us. Simply and plainly defined, leaders are people who have followers. They have earned recognition and respect."

The company's website provides the following description of its stated values:

> *"Servant-leaders are active listeners... they elicit trust... and share power. Basic Values are the most important characteristic of TDIndustries and guide all relationships.*
>
> • *Concern for and belief in individual human beings*
> • *Valuing individual differences*

49

- *Honesty*
- *Building trusting relationships*
- *Fairness*
- *Responsible behaviour*
- *High standards of business ethics"*

Jack Lowe Jr, past CEO of TDIndustries, was asked at a Greenleaf UK workshop in London a few years ago whether TDIndustries ever fired anyone. His answer was, of course they did! People sometimes broke the law, or didn't perform to the standard required. In the latter case, their managers would do everything they could to help them but ultimately lack of performance affected all employees and was a collective issue. He was also asked who set the strategy for the company, and his response was that it was the Board's role. Essentially, it was about trusting people to do their jobs fully – and this applied equally to Board members as to those carrying out the operational work. The key difference in a servant-leadership company is that all people are respected regardless of their job. Board members do not have higher status than other people doing other jobs. This can be tough on egos – servant-leadership isn't an easy way to lead! Jack Lowe, additionally, stresses the importance of gaining success by traditional standards. As he says: "It's got to be both; you've got to have a great place to work and run a great business, or hospital, or school."

What is remarkable about TDIndustries is its commitment to the servant-leadership values. Look at the mission statement – how many companies would put people in first place and mean it in terms of career opportunities? As Robert Greenleaf said, a leader's job is to grow people.

Synovus Financial

Synovus Financial is a diversified financial services holding company with more than $24 billion in assets based in Columbus, Georgia. It provides integrated financial services including banking, financial management, insurance, mortgage and leasing services through 40 affiliate banks and other Synovus offices in Georgia, Alabama, South Carolina, Florida and Tennessee. Synovus was voted the best company to work for in the USA in 1999. It has approximately 12,000 employees with assets of $33 billion. It is distinguished by its "culture of the heart". Its decision-making process starts with weighing up the **People** concerns **FIRST!** Again, this is unusual – in fact, almost unheard of for most companies.

The critical point to come from examining these servant-leadership companies is that it is possible both to focus on people and be highly successful. In fact, often the success has happened precisely because of the focus on people. However, servant-leadership companies are not just about putting people first – they focus as effectively on the other sides of organisational performance. For example, Southwest Airlines is one of the most efficient airlines in the world at turning around planes from landing to take-off. Performance and people go together and the superb servant-leadership companies recognise this and aim high! There are many parallels to Jim Collins' Level 5 leaders and their organisations. Collins famously wrote "Get the right people on the bus first, and then figure out where to drive it!"[18] In other words, get people on the bus first, then have them decide what needs to happen to go from good to great.

Given all these facts it would seem obvious that most organisations should adopt the servant-leadership approach if they want to be successful. The reasons why they don't are many, but chief among them would be ego and status. The subtitle of Greenleaf's book on servant-leadership is "A Journey into the Nature of Legitimate Power and Greatness". Anything that questions power can be seen as threatening. Also, servant-leadership is ultimately about a values approach to work, to leadership and others. You do it because you know it's the right thing to do – and you will then be successful. If you try servant-leadership just to make money it won't work, as the values will not be there to guide you through the tough times.

---

[18] Jim Collins, *Good to Be Great*, Random House, 2001

51

What can you do?

Robert Greenleaf is clear that:

> *"Organisation is the curiously neglected element. Thinking about it critically is not only avoided but sometimes it is spurned with some emotional heat. Perhaps this is because of an intuitive sense that trouble lies hidden there and we had best leave it alone and limp along with the tested and the tried, even though it may be archaic and inadequate."*[19]

In order to develop your organisation you need to start with **you**. What are your own values and strengths? How best do you serve people? This may be in a number of ways related to the organisational functions that were discussed earlier. You may be best at getting new business for the organisation, at handling contracts, at producing high quality goods, at helping people. Each of these ways of working can be seen as serving others.

So recognising your strengths and preferences is the first step. The second step is to understand and recognise the different and diverse contributions of others and encouraging them in their own path – not trying to impose your way on others. (A CEO I once met hired and fired a new Marketing Director within the space of a month. When I asked why, he said he wasn't doing any work. He was never in the office doing the marketing budgets as the CEO expected him to – he was always out talking to clients. The CEO apparently didn't understand that this was equally work!)

Next, look at your organisation. What is its moral purpose? How does it serve others? Nigel Springett has done research in the UK on mission statements of different companies. Those that had a purpose that focused on delivering value to customers were more likely to have successful business results than those that focused on maximising returns to shareholders.[20]

So what are your organisation's values and purpose? Are these

---

[19] Robert K. Greenleaf, ibid
[20] Nigel Springett, 'Corporate Purpose As the Basis of Moral Leadership of the Firm', *Strategic Change*, 2004

morally and ethically sound? Do they lead to congruent structures and processes that are true to these values? Are all areas and functions of the organisation equally honoured? To paraphrase Ghandi, "One man (or an organisation) cannot do right in one department of life while he (or the organisation) is occupied in doing wrong in any other department. Life is one indivisible whole."

	External to Organisation	
	2	1
Task	Does the organisation operate with clear principles in the market place? Does it compete in a fair and ethical manner? Does the organisation act in a responsible way with regard to the environment?	Is the organisation contributing to society as a whole? Is the organisation serving society in an ethical fashion? Does the organisation have a clear moral purpose?
	3	4
	Does the organisation aim to deliver a fair product or service for a fair price? Does it act in as efficient a way as possible to minimise its impact on the environment? Does it offer meaningful work for its employees?	Are employees treated with respect and trust? Are their highest priority needs being met? Are they growing as individuals?
	Internal to Organisation	

(Right side label: **People**)

Unilever's CEO for Russia and the Ukraine, Arjan Overwater, regards servant-leadership not just as the right thing to do but also as a business imperative. He sees servant-leadership as a highly effective management tool, as well as a moral compass for dealing with and reducing some of the crises we may face in today's world. He emphasises the need for reflection, for pinning down one's own morality and for having real conversations with people – not just slogans. They use the outdoors a lot as it helps people open up; they go on field trips to trek through villages and get to know their consumers. To quote Overwater on developing servant-leadership:

> *"Think of it as a road – a road to leadership. You need to consciously choose your moral principles. As I said at the beginning, all of you have unique gifts; you're very bright people. And this gives you an obligation to understand your moral calling. And be very close to people, very close to customers; it's something very simple and it's pays off. So here's my little sermon for today – each one of you sitting here needs to play a key role, because if we who have the means don't do it, nobody will do it."[21]*

---

[21] Unilever's CEO for Russia/Ukraine on 'How Servant-Leadership Benefits Everyone'

Applying Servant-Leadership

$$3$$

Servant-Leadership in a Professional Environment

Charlie Foote

Introduction

Despite the huge power and resources of the First World, we haven't achieved as much progress towards a better world as we should. What we have tried has often gone badly wrong. Even people with the best of intentions often produce results that make things worse.

We have a science and technology able to do unbelievable things, with a tremendous potential for doing more. But we are unable to agree on what should be done with this power and how we should do it. We have no science to answer the question, "Is this what we really want?"

The application of our technical resources to problems is done via *organisations* of one sort or another. These need to be led in the right direction and managed so that desired outcomes are achieved. In this respect, leadership and management are vital to the future.

We could argue that the application of power and resources to the best ends, taking into account the longer term as well as the shorter, could be described as a "wise" use of those resources. A number of thinkers are exploring this theme, and how organisations can be managed and controlled to get wise results. One of the first explorers in this field was Robert Greenleaf. His basic message is that using power in service gives good outcomes for everyone.

Adam Smith made the point that each butcher and baker, working from narrow self-interest, will make sure we are fed at a price we can afford. Many of us feel that this is too simplistic a view in a world of major multinational organisations, and a world where foreign aid enriches local rulers while having little or no effect on the poor for whom the aid was provided.

We often think of leaders as expecting to be served rather than serving others. Good leaders, of course, have always offered service to a noble cause. Greenleaf's concept allows discussion of leadership, and hence application of power, with proponents of other styles of leadership.

Leadership is accepted as a consequence of responsibility, not for its own sake. As leaders, we give service to our organisation's founding concept, to the people who work with us in achieving this concept, and to the people for whom the concept was devised – the "customers" of the concept.

Servant-leadership has inspired many practical people to set up organisations with a new outlook, and encouraged developments in training and management. From Greenleaf's source, new ideas are still constantly being generated. Ideas come from Greenleaf's concept rather like lava flowing from a volcano – some of this lava has settled and solidified in practical strategies and techniques, but more lava appears, and new ideas and techniques continue to be developed and introduced.

We introduced servant-leader concepts in our organisation

I helped to found a firm of Patent Attorneys in 1995, using the principles of servant-leadership. The firm grew very rapidly and is now in the top ten Patent Attorney firms in the UK.

The concept of servant-leadership led us to think about at what we were doing in the following three key areas:

- Focusing on the founding concept of the organisation
- Service to the people within the organisation
- Service to those served by the organisation ("customers" in the world of business)

We believed strongly in what we were doing, and we wanted to offer our products or services to as many people as practicably possible. This required us to make a profit.

We saw that making a profit was important for:

- Survival, to continue to serve people
- Expansion, to serve more people
- Attracting good people, to give and continue to give good service

Some people hear of servant-leadership and believe that it is about sacrificing profit to a noble aim. They consider it to be unrealistic in today's world. Those of us who practise servant-leadership know that this is not the case. Profit is vital, and we wanted to make a profit.

Service to the founding concept

By focusing on the founding concept of our organisation we removed narrow self-interest from our focus. The role of our organisation was to offer intellectual property services and that is what we did, and nothing else. We didn't try to enrich ourselves, gain political power, promote our family members or do anything else which sidetracked us from the goal of our firm. This focus, and the cleaner objectives which resulted from it, meant that our organisation did well, and this was reflected in our profit.

Service to the people in the organisation

We had a very strong desire to treat our colleagues with respect and value their contributions. Jobs were designed to be rewarding. We appreciated people and helped them to develop as workers and as people. The result of this was increased commitment and attention to the work that needed doing. We provided not just a good service but also a consistently good service. Absenteeism was small, and turnover of staff was very low – cutting down on induction and initial training costs.

People "turned up" intellectually. They brought their full attention to the job. They knew what they were doing to serve customers and the firm's founding concept, and they knew that they were appreciated for doing so. They were keen to look at what they were doing and make improvements; they knew they would not be criticised for using their brains, but encouraged. Such motivated people created excellent ideas.

We found, as we had hoped to find, that people who feel valued and supported are well placed to make customers feel valued and supported. Customer relations were very good.

Service to those served by the organisation

The clients whom our firm served were treated with dignity and respect, regardless of their size and financial importance to us. Treating clients well makes them value our services. Our output expanded though word of mouth, and we built up a reputation for service, honesty and integrity. Good service paid off.

Summary

These benefits accrued in practice. With our basis in servant-leadership we were successful and profitable.

Other benefits of the servant-leadership approach, like having happy and fulfilled employees, are hard to measure objectively, but we were certain they were operating in our firm to its overall benefit. It is reported that servant-leadership firms that are "great places to work" have economic performances that exceed the general economic performance of the local economy.

What did we actually do?

We aimed to provide excellent professional service as patent agents, but to do it in a certain style. We wanted to be a new sort of professional firm, based on fairness, equality, cooperation, and genuinely helping our clients and the people who worked with us.

We cut down the status differences between the different roles. We created partnership not as a position of privilege but one of obligation. We made significant efforts to help smaller clients, many of who were unclear about intellectual property and needed a lot of help. We felt that the intellectual property system is valuable to the country, and we wanted to help people use it. We intended to make a profit as a means to an end and not an end in itself.

We perceived some professionals as being greedy, and we often spoke about *not* being greedy when making decisions about the future of the firm. We wanted to share gains fairly. We accepted then, and still do, that it is not a practical proposition to pay everybody the same in a business like ours. But we aimed to keep our ratio of the highest paid to the lowest paid at about 10:1. Compare this with anything from 50:1 upwards in a typical firm of commercial lawyers. We saw, and still see, cooperation as a way for everyone to gain. We always aimed to cooperate, with staff and with clients, for the mutual benefit of all. In practical terms we included everyone in decisions, and had a stated aim of always trying to achieve consensus.

Finally, we wanted to have fun. We wanted to enjoy our work, feel good about what we were doing and create pleasure for others and ourselves.

We had clear values, as set out above. Perhaps the values can be summarised as:

- Profit for a reason, not an end in itself
- Integrity in all dealings
- Openness and transparency
- Equality
- Mutual respect between colleagues, clients and all people
- No greed or narrow selfish motives

These were verbal agreements between the founders. We had various written versions of it to show new joiners, but it was fundamentally verbal.

Here are some of the practical steps, which followed from these principles:

- Internal meetings were open to everyone.
  *In fact we **invited** everyone at first; only when the meetings started to get very big did we leave it to personal choice*

- The reward system respected individual contributions to some extent, but had a large weighting towards shared reward.

- Decisions were made by consensus.
  For example, we consulted everyone when we decided on new premises.

- Fees were set at what seemed fair levels, rather than what would bring us the greatest profit.

- We encouraged rapid entry into the partnership for qualified people.

Realised benefits of implementation

Here are some of the realised benefits of our approach.

Engagement and commitment

We found that people really support a firm founded on servant-leader principles. Our aim was to provide meaningful jobs and in practice people really enjoyed them.

We had a very flat hierarchy. People were encouraged to do their jobs without supervision once they knew what the firm was trying to do and how their roles fitted into that. Everybody had the same terms and conditions. Our people had full a say in their own destinies, and could develop as people. They enjoyed helping others and they enjoyed themselves.

Not surprisingly, people mostly loved this sort of working environment and they made important contributions to the firm's growth and success. They were motivated and engaged, they gave their attention and effort, they gave their ideas, and they stayed with us.

We chose not to give additional incentives to hard work and good performance other than being part of the firm, but the response was excellent. We deliberately chose not to pay overtime, telling people that they should have a life outside work – but people gave their overtime for nothing in the few cases where it was needed. We did not believe in, or use any performance-related pay, except in the broad sense that effective people were promoted, and paid more.

Everyone working in the firm enjoyed the work and liked the firm. People did not often leave us, and hence we did not lose the valuable experience that was built up as the firm developed.

We did not, thankfully, have any crises, but when times of tension arrived we were all happy to work hard and creatively put things right. Thus the organisation felt resilient – able to cope effectively with big changes.

Growth and development

Patent Attorneys provide a service and it was important to us that we provided a good service. We wanted our clients to feel listened to and helped, to feel that we wanted them to enjoy interacting with us. By treating our own people well, we encouraged an attitude in which our clients were treated well. Those employees feeling well served themselves gave excellent service to customers, so the business grew and developed. Our growth was based on the formation of relationships.

This was real, solid, long-term growth. We grew very rapidly under a servant-leader approach, achieving compound growth at over 50% for the first seven years of operation.

Low staff turnover

We lost very few people in the first five years. In fact, it was a major shock to us when anyone left – even if they had reasons outside work for doing so.

63

Pleasant working environment

We all enjoyed going to work. People enjoyed work without close management, being able to do things their own way. Those of us with a management role were able to help and coach rather than give orders, and we enjoyed working with engaged people. The management role was more concerned with helping and supporting than with direction and monitoring. In my experience, people are happier and more productive under servant-leadership than more traditional 'command and control' structures.

Problems of implementation

We now believe that servant-leadership requires work and vigilance to make it work. There may have to be a large shake-up in people's thinking for them to fully accept the concept of servant-leadership. Some people do not thrive in a servant-leadership environment. It has been noted that, when a prime mover in an area using servant-leadership moves on, servant-leadership sometimes begins to fade out. A new champion cannot always be found. This is often because potential successors do not have a background in servant-leadership – and even where they do, it does take effort to introduce and maintain the new approach, against conventional wisdom, and some people are just not ready to take this on. If a firm has been in operation long enough, with commitment to servant-leadership, there will be internal candidates who don't need to be taught the concept. Home-grown leaders are the best solution.

We implemented a servant-leader approach when we set up our firm. Unfortunately, we saw it diffused in later years. One of the reasons for this related to our accepting new people too readily into the partnership, where every partner had an equal vote. This ultimately had the effect of biasing the attitude within the firm from being very servant-leadership based towards being more traditional – mainly because the new people did not really understand what we were trying to achieve (they had not learned by being there as our approach developed). Although the firm remains highly successful, there has been a modification of the original impetus, and the atmosphere in the firm has changed.

These are some of the problems we came up against. They are avoidable if you know about them in advance and here are a few tips on what we would do if we started again.

Values drift

Values have a tendency to drift.

How does this happen?

Sometimes people took actions without thinking them through in relation to the values, and these actions implied a change in values.

Some strategic decisions which we made were rather borderline. Rather than stick strictly to our values, we allowed them to change slightly to allow the new opportunity to fit within them.

In our case we found that people who joined us sometimes experienced the values in a way that they did not expect, and then tried to ignore them or change them. We felt people had a "right" to join us, even if they didn't share our values – this was a part of our equality/democracy. We thought that after being with us for a while people would be converted to the approach even if they didn't believe in it when they joined. I now believe we were misguided in both these views.

In another implementation we would much more actively resist any drift in values. Firstly we would be very specific about the firm's values. They would be unambiguously written, and 100% agreed in advance of joining. Those joining would be told that they must live by the values, or they would be asked to re-educate or move on.

Secondly, we would be much more selective about who we employed – not accepting people who would not fit in with the firm's values, however well qualified in other ways.

Thirdly, we would have regular training sessions in what we were trying to do – something we clearly neglected in the past.

The butterfly turns back into the caterpillar

Narrow self-interest has a strong tendency to rear its head. The butterfly is mobile, has beauty, breeds and sups nectar. It is a fine symbol of a servant-leader – dedicated to service. The caterpillar, however, is a material being – it relentlessly chews leaves and builds up its personal resources.

We found that many people perceived servant-leadership as not taking into account their short-term selfish needs. They wanted more money and status – and our system did not give it to them. They were prepared to see service to others as an aim, but only to a point. When they felt that they needed more money they would say that servant-leadership was failing them. We tolerated this – in future, I would ask people with these differing values and objectives to go get their extra money elsewhere.

We accepted the wrong people into our ranks

In my firm, we let anybody join who said that they accepted our values. We trusted people from the very start.

We discovered that people mislead you to get the job. Whether deliberate (and I think this is unusual) or unwitting a few people have told us at interview that they fully supported the firm's values and, as soon as they joined us they started to work against them. They have claimed that they were never told what the true situation was – of course they were, but they did not listen or perhaps were simply unable to take it in.

In future we would be much more careful in the selection process. If that meant a shortage of good people, we would be prepared to grow more slowly while waiting for the right people to appear.

Fear and conventional wisdom

We found that some people became very fearful when they took the responsibility that arose from their work. In this state of fearfulness they tended to revert to the "conventional" ways of doing things. They said things like "I want people to do as I tell them – I am in charge", and "This is the way things work – this is the way businesses have always run."

Perhaps through our lack of an internal training programme they tended to fall back on methods they had seen others use in other organisations, rather than following the more equality-based approach which we favoured. As soon as they became scared of their responsibility, they stopped listening and we found it hard to guide them down our route.

Education about servant-leadership, as a part of everyone's employment with us, would have helped us diffuse this problem.

Final thoughts

Here are some thoughts on leadership and management resulting from our experience.

Hierarchy

Servant-leadership is neutral to hierarchy – it is not "against" hierarchy. It is against some of the attitudes which have traditionally gone with hierarchy – command, control, and orders. It is against replacing initiative and responsibility by obedience to unexplained orders.

It is hard to imagine a large commercial organisation without at least some hierarchy. Hierarchy increases efficiency, particularly in a static environment. A large company without any hierarchy would be too inefficient to operate. But too much hierarchy can make a firm inflexible and unresponsive to the marketplace.

A good hierarchy can be flat, and that can help overcome problems. We would say that a better way forward is to make your (minimal) hierarchy a hierarchy of levels of *operation* rather than a hierarchy of levels of *status* and *privilege*.

Leadership

Servant-leaders seek to serve, and accept leadership as a consequence of that. They realise that they are the best people to take on the role, and may do it rather reluctantly. This is very different from the traditional leadership model where people aspire to lead and to be described as "born leaders". People who want the power and prestige associated with leadership are often poor leaders. We were highly suspicious of "born leader" types, especially as they always saw what we were trying to do as "directionless" and wanted to impose their "direction" which they seemed to believe we could not do without!

Guiding principles

All firms have guiding principles whether they are written down or not. A new employee will get his or her antennae out and establish "how things operate around there" before making any moves. They are picking up the guiding principles.

Servant-leaders believe in making guiding principles explicit. And they also want them to be broadly moral. This is not a religious inspiration but a combination of a desire for fairness and a reluctance to support activities that do harm.

Servant-leaders stick to their values and expect their colleagues to stick to them also – so the organisation becomes "values driven". A number of people have said to us that during the running of any business you have to change your values if circumstances change. This reflects a fundamental misunderstanding of the nature of values, and is absolutely contrary to the principles of servant-leadership. It reminds me of the Hollywood mogul who addressed a meeting as follows: "Gentlemen, these are my principles. But if you don't like them I have others."

We may have to change the things we do, or the way we do things, but we do not want to change the values underlying the actions.

Personal development

People want to develop themselves. This is not their first priority, but once they are earning adequate amounts of money, and they feel that they are in a job, which adds meaning to their lives, and to which they can feel a sense of belonging, then personal development becomes important. We found this to be true. We found we could encourage our colleagues in this by recognising their talents and helping them find more demanding and rewarding roles within the organisation.

Reward systems

We started from the premise that more than money motivates people. Some of the other things that motivate people are:

- Time to enjoy their families – holiday entitlement, restricted overtime, etc.
- Being cared for – health insurance, pension provision, etc.
- Clarity in what they are doing – what and why, and how good work is judged
- A good working atmosphere – coming to work is enjoyable
- Feeling valued – given real jobs and recognition for doing them well
- Opportunities for advancement – promotion prospects
- Opportunities to contribute – being listened to; suggestion schemes

Put together this is a great offer to employees. We found that we did not have to pay over the odds to attract and retain people.

Enlightened self-interest

Servant-leaders get pleasure from helping their colleagues to develop, and gain satisfaction from it. But there is a longer-term factor, which should not be forgotten – enlightened self-interest.

If our people are happy in their work, and are increasing their talents and qualification, they will do better work. They will feel better about themselves, and the firm will operate better – being more efficient and productive and having a better reputation in the marketplace. The founding concept will spread, hopefully to the benefit of all.

Servant-leadership is against narrow self-interest but not against enlightened self-interest. A better world for you is also a better world for me – so let's go forward together.

4

Servant-Leadership: A CEO's Perspective

Bob Henry

My overall perspective

As individuals we will have our own perspective or *'our truth'* as to what the term servant-leadership means to us. An important starting point from my perspective is in relation to the question that is often asked when I talk to other people about servant-leadership, particularly when those others are 'leaders' of their organisation. The question asked is, *"So what is this servant-leadership stuff all about, then?"* And my reply is often another question, always a good tactic, and that question is, *"What do you think your leadership is in service of?"*

Why that question? Well, my take on this is that if your leadership is in service of yourself rather than of others, that is probably more about your personal desire for power and authority. If your leadership is in service of others, then for me this is more what servant-leadership is about.

Another way of looking at that question is to ask what is the intent behind your leadership and what impact are you seeking to achieve? So, in writing about servant-leadership from the perspective of a CEO I will try and keep that question to the fore: *"What is my intent and what am I seeking to impact on?"*

This may not always fit with the accepted definition or view of servant-leadership, but does that really matter? For me it is the spirit of the intention that is important rather than a rigid adherence to a principle. Why is that important? Well, in my experience rigid adherence to a principle, rather than the spirit of intent, is usually quickly followed by the establishment of dogma – i.e. trying to force your beliefs on others – which seems to me to run counter to the wish to provide service to others.

I had a view that if I was ever in a position where I could significantly influence the environment in which I and others worked, it would be an environment that was built on involvement, participation and individual development – that it would be an open and fully participative community driven by a strong desire to provide service to others, whether internal or external to the organisation.

This seems to fit reasonably well with Robert Greenleaf's view that *"the first order of business is to build a group of people who, under the influence of the institution, grow taller and become healthier, stronger and more autonomous."*

Finally, in this introduction I think it is important to put servant-leadership in context with other styles or concepts of leadership. From my perspective, servant-leadership is the bedrock of my leadership. From that position I may well engage in what may be recognised as more traditional leadership 'styles' – e.g. charismatic leadership, transactional leadership, transformational leadership, etc. However it is the intent of servant-leadership that determines how and what I enact when using a variety of styles – flexibility being a key aspect of leadership.

What do I mean by enact?

What I mean by this is that it is all well and good to espouse our thoughts and beliefs about servant-leadership, participation, self-empowerment, and so on, but what does it actually mean in practice? Again I can only speak from my own perspective. I can only talk about what I have done, and in doing so I am not saying there is a right or wrong way, only that it is my way. So what I will attempt to do in the remainder of this chapter is to detail some of my espoused theories with what I actually did as a CEO – i.e. what I enacted. For me this is an important and fundamental position. If you espouse one thing but then enact another, the whole integrity of your leadership is undermined. This will often be difficult, as a varied number of pressures will be exerted both by self on self and others on self that will seek to try and get you to act in a way that is at odds with what you espouse.

An example of this for me was when I made the transition from being an Operations Director to Chief Executive Officer. I was moving to a position where I was ultimately accountable for the success of the business, and the temptation when one is in that position of accountability is that you think you have to control everything. If you are accountable, surely you have to control everything, otherwise how can you accept the accountability? Clearly this is nonsense as it implies that:

- I must know everything, which is clearly beyond most mortals. (I have to know enough and I have to rely on the expertise and trustworthiness of others.)

- I must be able to control every aspect of the business. (In my view control is often an illusionary position we put ourselves in when we don't have confidence in others.)

It is difficult for someone with an operations background to accept that they can be accountable without absolute control of all the resources in the organisation, but clearly, following the position of Greenleaf (*"the first order of business is to build a group of people who, under the influence of the institution, grow taller and become healthier, stronger and more autonomous"*), that is exactly the position one needs to accept. It requires you to recognise the complex nature of the organisational system and realise that believing you can control its every move is an illusion.

In practice, that required me to challenge every instance where someone was asking me to take a decision. The challenge is always twofold; in the first instance the challenge is why does the individual believe that they cannot make the decision themselves, and in the second instance, it is a challenge of my own need to make decisions as I feel myself lurching towards making the decision for the other person, whether they need me to do that or not.

This requires you to explore and inquire with the other person what valid restrainers are in place that make them feel they are unable to take the decision. Do they have the required level of competency? Do they feel they do not have the autonomy, that some policy requires my consent, etc.? You need to be supportive rather than prescriptive in this inquiry process, the purpose of which is to encourage the individual to understand the level of autonomy they really have. At the other end of the spectrum, of course, this may be a decision that only I could make as the CEO, but at least that will be clear and avoids me just rushing in and making decision that I don't need to make. Sure, it takes a bit of time in the first instance; just making the decision may seem quick, but not if the individual keeps coming back to you to make decisions that they could legitimately make. That can become very time-consuming.

Accessibility is key

I believe that a key aspect of the practice of servant-leadership is to be accessible to everyone in the organisation and not create a set of artificial barriers between yourself and those you are seeking to support. You also need to be aware that others will seek to put these barriers in place even though you don't desire them. Here is an example of what I mean. Often in organisations you find the CEO is 'protected' by having his own private office to which access by others is usually controlled by the CEO's PA. This will happen regardless of what the CEO intends, because the organisational view is that we need to filter the access to the CEO to make sure they are not unnecessarily bothered by people impinging on their time. Changing this organisational view can be quite difficult, and it won't happen merely because the CEO announces that he has an open door policy. You must actually do something significant to get what you espouse to happen.

In my case, I did away with my private office and the specific PA role, and located myself in the one of the open office spaces, thinking

73

that people will now have virtually unfettered access to me. How wrong I was! What I noticed was that there was some increase in contact but what I also noticed was that the pervading organisational view was that, despite my protestations, I needed my own space and so I noticed over a very short space of time that a range of filing cabinets started to surround 'my space' effectively isolating me from the others in the open office. Subsequently I determined that I needed to do something more specific if I was create an atmosphere of real open access, and so I relocated myself again to a space in the main reception area of the office, a space that could not be 'fenced in'. My reasoning for choosing that location is that everyone has to pass through the reception area at some time during the day, so I couldn't be avoided. It also meant I was more accessible to customers and other visitors to the organisation, which was a real advantage in understanding what those external to the organisation were expecting from us in the way of service, where that expectation was not being met and, as importantly, where it was being met or exceeded.

One might think that everyone would appreciate the move, and that might be a logical expectation from a servant-leadership perspective. Your leadership is in service to others, but not necessarily from the more traditional perspective of leadership where the purpose of others is to serve the leader. What I had not appreciated was how strong the traditional hierarchical paradigm can be in an organisation. Whilst I was happy with a greater degree of openness and autonomy, and therefore expected everyone else would also welcome it, I was wrong! Actually, many found it to be a great threat and very unsettling; they may not have liked the previous leadership style but at least they knew what it was. They had developed ways of working to it, and then along comes this new CEO, this lunatic, who is talking about greater openness, more decisions being taken upwards rather than from the top downwards, going straight to people without going through the management structures, and so on. Managers suddenly feel their 'authority' being undermined, and people might suddenly find themselves being talked to directly by the CEO, at their desk, not his, being asked questions about what they do. Very unsettling.

So, what the system tries to do is to pull you back into the way it was before, and that is so frustrating as, of course, you are making these changes for their benefit not yours. Or was I? Maybe it was more about me trying to impose on others my beliefs about how an organisation should be led and operated, so when I was doing this openness, supportive and accessible stuff was I really doing it for the benefit of others or myself? In truth, I believe my intention was to lead from the standpoint of servant-leadership, but by imposing it on others the impact was the opposite. In other words I was not enacting what I espoused. More importantly, I was not making my intentions and the impact that I was seeking clear to people, assuming they would understand that from what I was doing.

So, another key learning point: never assume that people will understand what your intention is merely through your actions. You need to be extremely clear about your intentions, and check frequently the understanding of others. Also seek to understand how it fits with their current world-view of the organisation, and how that world-view will be impacted on as you move to a more servant-leadership style of leading.

In the end we got there. Over time, people could see that I was enacting what I was espousing despite the various setbacks and despite continuing pressure to revert to a more 'conventional' style of leadership. They could see I was sticking with it.

Leading by example

Another important lesson I learnt is that you cannot force others to adopt servant-leadership as their style of leadership. The fact that I have a firm belief that it seems the 'right way of leading' doesn't mean it has to be adopted by all. In fact, my experience was that the more challenging others were of my style, the healthier the situation. Why do I think that? Well, as a CEO you have a particular status within an organisation, and associated with that status can be a feeling among employees that whatever the CEO thinks is right and must be copied or supported to some degree or other by everyone in the organisation. I think that is a potentially dangerous path to follow. I would like, but not insist, that others would come to realise the benefits to self and the organisation of being more servant-leader oriented in their leadership behaviours. You can lead by displaying the behaviours that underpin your leadership style. Lead by example, but in doing so, be very aware that certainly in the initial stages people will be looking for you to revert to what they had previously experienced. They can then say, *"There you are, it didn't take long before he showed his true colours. I knew all that talk of openness and support was too good to be true."*

So be aware in your leading by example that you are also going to set a bad example sometimes – i.e. you are not going to enact what you espouse.

Recognising that, and being totally honest with yourself and others that this has happened is, I think, critical in maintaining your integrity as a servant-leader. Being able to do this 'in the moment' is a really helpful skill to develop. It requires a high level of self-awareness, and by that I mean recognising at the time what effect your behaviour is having on the immediate situation. It is far more helpful to recgonise this while it is happening than to reflect on it some time in the future. Why is that particularly helpful? Well, if you reflect and act on it in the future, whilst that might be useful, you have lost the opportunity to change what might happen in the here in now. An example of this would be when I realised, as I was doing it, that I was reacting badly in a particular situation and then voiced that I realised that that was what I was doing. For instance, I had been encouraging people to make decisions without reference to me, and I was sitting in a meeting where people were telling me subsequently about a decision they had made. I found my self getting quite annoyed and being rather confrontational about why they had decided on that course of action.

I realised that I was behaving that way because I felt this was a decision they should have involved me in, and I was missing the whole point about whether it was a good decision or not. It had become about my need to be involved. Once I acknowledged that, I was able to voice why I was not behaving in an appropriate way and that it was not about the fact they had made the decision, it was about me feeling left out and acknowledging that they were right not to have included me. My doing that at the time and in the moment meant we were all able to have a much more productive conversation than if I had continued to behave badly. By reflecting on this at some future time and then maybe discussing it with those involved might be helpful at one level but what it will not have done is actually enable a better outcome at the time.

Another example was when I relocated to the open office, and subsequently to the reception area, I did not insist that other senior directors/managers do the same. My experience was that regardless of whatever they individually did in this respect, the overall atmosphere in the organisation would become more open and supportive of people in the organisation, and externally to other stakeholders and clients. I think individuals shifted significantly in their behaviours whilst at the same time they were able to do so at their own pace and because they were seeing the benefits of doing so rather than being forced to make a change.

Eventually this open and supportive set of behaviours became the norm throughout the majority of the organisation; a new paradigm was established. Interestingly, at that stage the internal perspective was that 'this is just the way we work' and is no great thing. At the same time, externally people would notice something was different and often the comment made by external stakeholders or visitors was that they noticed within a short time of either visiting the office or contacting us that the people they dealt with seemed to want to help them and were interested in them and their needs. Sure, this did not happen all the time for everyone, but it happened with significant frequency to be indicative of the general behaviour of the organisation.

Following on from this, we were frequently visited by other organisations that were interested in what we were doing, and looking to see if there were lessons for them that they might take back to their own operations.

Being clear what conversation you are in

One thing about closed organisations is that you are normally pretty clear about what sort of conversation you are in. It might, for example, be a 'doing' conversation where you are being told what to do or what not to do – or perhaps a 'blaming' conversation focusing on who is to blame or why you are to blame.

In an open organisation – and, by default, I think organisations that are servant-leadership orientated are open – being clear about the nature of the conversation you are in can become more problematic. This is particularly so for the CEO of an open organisation, where it is very easy to make assumptions about the type of conversation you are in at any one time. If we take the situation where I am either walking around in the office or sitting in the reception area, then conversations are often going to take place in an informal way ('just passing by'). There are no artefacts or symbols to indicate the type of conversation you or others want to have, unlike being called into the CEO's office where some indication of the type of conversation you are about to have is signalled in advance.

Let's assume for the purpose of illustration that there are three basic types of conversation that take place between a CEO and others:

- **Looking for a decision** – the individual is actually looking for you as the CEO to take a decision.
- **Exploring options** – the individual wants to explore some options about a future course of action but doesn't want you to necessarily make a decision; they may merely be seeking an opinion.
- **Thinking aloud** – the individual wants to be able to think out aloud, perhaps share some blue-sky thinking, and the last thing they want is a decision; they are only looking for a 'thinking partner'.

Let's say that the last conversation you had with an individual was one where a decision was needed, and now you find yourself in a subsequent conversation and it is not made clear at the outset the nature of the conversation that the individual wants on this occasion. There is a risk that you will assume that since the last time you spoke they were looking for a decision, this is what they want from this subsequent conversation. However, in this conversation they merely want to bounce around some options or ideas so they can get a view from you, and then subsequently they will make any decision. So they start to discuss some options but you think they want a decision, so you take their options and then give them a decision – i.e. this is what you should do! As CEO you feel OK in that you have met your perceived need that they are looking for a decision; they are thinking, *"How did that happen? I only wanted to talk over some options, now I have been told what to do – that wasn't what I wanted, but hey, it is the CEO, so I better get on with implementing the decision".*

I firmly believe that the responsibility for clarifying the nature of the conversation lies with you as the CEO, and that this should happen in the opening seconds of the conversation. If you are initiating the conversation with someone then be very clear up front what your intention is for this conversation, and what outcome you are expecting from it. If the other person has initiated the conversation, and they have not given that clarity of expectation early on in the conversation, then you need to ask them to clarify what type of conversation they want on this occasion and what is the expected outcome they are seeking. Once this becomes the norm in conversational terms (i.e. clarity of intent and expectation), then you find organisational conversation becomes much more productive and there is less opportunity for assumptions to be made and hence less poor communication.

The 'law of the unexpected outcome'

One of the outcomes you would expect following Robert Greenleaf's vision of servant-leadership (*"the first order of business is to build a group of people who, under the influence of the institution, grow taller and become healthier, stronger and more autonomous"*), is that people will find themselves more often in situations where they have the autonomy to make decisions. That means that sometimes they are going to make decisions that result in things not quite turning out the way they had expected. In many organisations this is known as making a mistake!

I prefer to take the view as a CEO that, in general, individuals do not set out to make mistakes; in fact, it usually the very opposite – they set out to achieve a result that will be of benefit to others. I also have a distinct dislike of the term *'a blame-free culture'*, as that can often be misinterpreted as meaning it is OK to keep making mistakes, which is not a helpful behaviour in my view. So we use this phrase of *'the law of the unexpected outcome'* which works as follows.

This law is predicated on the assumption that people will make decisions based on the best of intentions and available information, and that they expect a certain outcome or result to come out of making that decision. What can happen on occasions is that the expected outcome is not achieved, and there is an unexpected outcome. The law states that this is acceptable as long as the reasons why the unexpected outcome arose are explored and shared with others so that it becomes widely known that, given this set of circumstances and actions again in the future, this sort of outcome could be expected to occur. That means that if someone repeats the same actions in the same or similar circumstances the outcome can no longer be unexpected, indeed it should be expected and that is not acceptable behaviour.

On occasions when this happens, you will feel a great urge to tear your hair out! Surely when they took that decision they could have expected this to happen; how could they have been that stupid or unaware? Well, for a start, they are not you; they will have arrived at that decision based on their knowledge and assumptions, not yours, and they will have taken it for the best of reasons. I have made plenty of 'sub-optimal' decisions as a CEO, but at the time I made them I thought they were the right decisions. It is only subsequently that this turned out not to be the case. As CEO you need to be very open about your 'mistakes' – again, follow the dictum of enacting what you espoused to others, being open and therefore feeling vulnerable. Whilst it can be uncomfortable, it is no bad thing.

Keeping redundancy in the system

This may seem a peculiar concept, since many organisations seem intent on taking out all redundancy from within the organisation. Sometimes there may be overriding reasons why redundancy has to be taken out of the organisation, but often it may be the first choice rather than seeing what opportunities keeping redundancy can offer. What do I mean by this? If we take an example, such as improvement in efficiency through the introduction of new technology or changes in working practices that might lead to a reduction in the number of people needed in the future, accepted practice might be to make that number of people redundant, and take them out of the organisation – 'letting people go', as it is sometimes presented. An alternative view, and one that experience has often shown to me to produce a better outcome, is to hold on to that redundancy, and see it as an opportunity to use it for something else – like growing new business. Often in organisations we have little spare capacity to innovate and pursue new opportunities; by keeping redundancy in the system as the first option rather taking it out as the first option gives you that flexibility. As a CEO that was always my first position – i.e. let's see what we can do that we couldn't do previously, let's see what opportunities can come out of this. Even more productive in my experience was to encourage those who would have been otherwise redundant, to see what new opportunities for innovation and business growth they could themselves create. In my experience, I never once regretted taking that stance; it always produced results. You just have to take the risk in the first instance.

Why bother with all this servant-leadership stuff?

Intuitively for me it feels right. It makes absolute sense to me that if people are supported and developed, able to realise their full potential and able to be more autonomous on a day-to-day basis, then the organisation will provide a superior service and deliver improved bottom line performance. At the end of the day an organisation needs to perform and develop, otherwise it will cease to exist and just being idealistic without being pragmatic is the road to decline.

I have often had people say to me when I have talked about how we operate as an organisation, that it all sounds a bit idealistic, and my response is always that it is only idealistic if you talk about it but don't do it! As soon as you enact it, then it ceases to be idealistic and becomes the ideal, and experience has shown that bottom line results significantly improve, both financially and in service delivery terms. There are plenty of other examples in other organisations where servant-leadership exists as the organisational paradigm, and these organisations flourish and produce consistently good results.

Summing up

I am not sure that my interpretation of the concept and practice of servant-leadership is one that others would recognise but, as I have already said, in my view it is the intention and spirit one adopts that is probably the most important aspect of one's leadership, and hopefully you at least have a sense of my intent around my leadership.

Clearly, there are a wide range of other attributes around leadership that one could adopt, but I think I have identified the key ones for me as a CEO, and I would like to think they make sense to others. So now is probably a good time to summarise these:

- Be clear about your intentions and the impact you wish to have on others and situations.
- Ensure that you enact what you espouse, and recognise when you are not doing that; be open and honest with others when this is the case. Lead by example even though that may make you feel vulnerable at times.
- Make yourself accessible to others; don't believe that by saying you have an open door policy, others will believe it. You have to act in a way that will make you accessible.
- Be clear about the nature of each individual conversation you initiate and ask others about their conversational intentions when they initiate the conversation you find yourself in.

- Develop something like the 'law of unexpected outcomes' to enable people to take risks and share learning about when that doesn't quite work out.
- Keep some redundancy in the organisation and see it as an opportunity rather than a problem.

5

Servant-Leadership Through Engagement

Andrew Walsh

The following chapter outlines the trials, tribulations and rewards of an organisation which uses servant-leadership in its core philosophy.

The Pensions Trust is an occupational pension business for charities and not-for-profit organisations. It's an organisation like many others, a small to medium sized enterprise (SME) with 250 employees based on three sites in the UK. As Head of Business Resources at the Trust, I see servant-leadership as something of a philosophy – a way of life, an all-encompassing approach. It's not a management tool, which can be bolted onto a business strategy; rather it can be applied to the management of businesses with stunningly good effect. I have sought to take the spirit of servant-leadership and apply it in a very practical way to a business.

For some organisations, a servant-leadership approach has been inherent because the owner is him/herself a servant-leader. But for other organisations it represents a tough change in the way things are done. It's not easy and it's not very comfortable to some, at least not at first. Despite some of the frustrations and challenges of the approach, I am still a big fan of servant-leadership. For a concept which is so simple, to be able to change the way people perform and behave so dramatically never fails to amaze me.

Almost inevitably, a change towards a servant-leadership approach in a business has to be linked with the need for change anyway. It could be born out of crisis (change or die), or because a new business strategy is adopted (change to keep up). The Pensions Trust has embraced servant-leadership as part of a need to change in order to compete and to be successful.

What sort of change was needed? Well, it's the usual story – the need for better customer service, more efficiency, and better productivity. Why the change was needed related to the market in which the Trust operates. The Pensions Trust is an occupational pension scheme for charities, voluntary organisations and the not-for-profit sector. There had been great expansion over previous 15 years, but this had slowed down by 2005 to disappointing growth levels. Why was this slowing down happening? Well, the Trust started asking its customers, and they cited the loss of confidence by employees in the pensions market in general and the arrival of serious competition to an otherwise niche market.

The Trust had to do some serious thinking about how to continue to grow and prosper.

As a result, the business spent a great deal of time and effort defining a new business strategy. This took account of the fact that although it operates in the charitable sector for customers, the Trust's competition for products, services and labour was in the financial services sector.

This was always a difficult balance for leaders and managers in the business. The Trust concluded that the way it competed was not on price alone, but on quality in terms of product, service and customer care. As a mutual organisation (i.e. owned by its members) the Trust decided to position itself as the champion of pensions in the charitable sector, totally trustworthy, and honest with really good value products.

"We don't sell pensions," they said. "We sell quality of life in retirement for relatively low paid people."

This was formalised in 2005/6 and to support this strategy I was charged with spearheading a new people strategy to support it. I developed what I called the "ASDA/Aga" test to decide what type of workforce was needed to carry forward the business strategy.

At one extreme the ASDA style was reflected by a business

driven heavily by price and economies of scale. The type of workforce needed for a successful supermarket chain would be:

- Well trained to so their job according to an agreed process
- Generally skilled according to the job they do
- Proud of what they do
- Geared towards clinical customer care
- Rewarded according to sales
- Given lots of non work related benefits – work social clubs, etc.

At the other end, luxury oven manufacturer Aga was not driven heavily by price. It sold a way of life and experience, rather than just an oven. Price was actually relatively unimportant. The type of workforce for this type of organisation, I argued, was very different: All employees needed to:

- Be passionate about what the business produces
- Know about all aspects of the business at all levels
- Be multi-skilled to do many different roles
- Be proud of what the business does
- Understand how they contribute to the business
- Be geared towards extraordinary customer care
- Be rewarded according to quality of work rather than quantity

At the Trust they decided that they were definitely more Aga, and that the principle strategic theme would be to get and keep a workforce full of engaged people. Such people were the only ones who could really deliver that type of work force.

Of course, we all know what engaged people are like – ask anyone and they will be able to name someone who is engaged at work, or serving behind the bar, or in a shop, or at a call centre. But if the Trust was to get a workforce made up of engaged people it was going to need a more structured definition of what "engaged" means.

They got the workforce to define what engagement meant and the results were along the lines of the following:

Understands why the Trust is here and what it stands for
Is passionate about the Business
Does what they say they are going to do
Takes responsibility/ownership for their own actions
Is conscientious and punctual
Takes the initiative to develop themselves in all areas
Carries out discretionary activity on behalf of the team and the Trust
Demonstrates a "can do" approach
Is positive and enthusiastic about the work
Responds constructively to change
Is proactive and looks for improvement in line with team and business goals
Supports the team and the Trust
Questions, participates and is happy to be questioned
Actively demonstrates the Trust's values and ethos
Cares about and takes pride in his/her work

The real challenge is providing the cultural environment for people to become and stay engaged. My team and I did some more research among our people to find out what makes people behave in this engaged way. The results were interesting. Managers' behaviour seemed to be the biggest influencer of individuals' engagement by far. This was backed up by external surveys – one, by Towers Perrin, is shown at the end of this chapter.

Even more interesting was the response from employees who were already seen as engaged. They went further and cited which management behaviour engaged them, and what they described was uncannily how a servant-leader manages. So, the Trust set out on its journey to develop managers and leaders who could engage their teams using a servant-leader approach.

I believe that the principle of servant-leadership is that managers facilitate the team to get on with the job. They provide the tools, the environment, make sure the budgets are sorted, and ensure that appropriate authority is given, so people can get on with doing it. Then they stand back. The team members know best how to deal with customers; they know what's wrong with the processes.

The Pensions Trust doesn't actually call its approach servant-leadership – I am never big on labels because they tend to imply that it's a management tool, which it isn't. However the people strategy is quite clear in its approach to management style. The overriding culture at the Trust is that managers inspire and facilitate team members to enable them to do the job in the way they (the team members) think best serves the customer, subject to overall standards.

With managers serving the team rather than directing them, we find we unleash a huge amount of knowledge, skills and application, which directly increases productivity.

Here's an example in practice. Early on in the process the Trust held a series of sessions for all the workforce in teams of five or six to discuss the business and people strategies. They were charged with coming up with an image of what the Trust would be like in 2010 according to the business strategy. This was to be in a creative format, such as a picture, a song, a play or a sculpture. This in itself was unusual for the Trust, but more unusual still was the fact that the managers acted as facilitators rather than leaders for each team. They were asked to serve the teams by making sure that they knew what they were being asked to do, and to stock up on materials if required, get cups of coffee for the team, and so on.

The results were staggering – normally conservative, safe, risk-adverse pensions people came up with creative and innovative ideas, which were remarkable. Short plays, songs and even dances were represented.

Managers were astonished at the innovation within their teams, but all agreed that it had been really hard not to lead and direct the groups. As one said: "Serving the group just didn't feel like managing."

In practical terms this means we are asking our managers to let go of their egos and to delegate real responsibility, not just tasks – to allow team members to innovate, create, decide and influence at all levels of the business. This makes them passionate about the business and proud of what they do, and they then apply what we call discretionary effort on behalf of the business.

I remember a great example of this. The Trust produced standard letters of response to regular occurrences, such as a change of address, transfer of pensions or death of a member. These were typically put together by managers, and the Pensions Administrators filled in details of dates, names, etc. As the new culture was rolling out, one of the Pensions Assistants, the most junior members of our team, challenged one of the standard letters saying that it was not actually in line with our values and should be rewritten. And he was right. A revised style was adopted which was more customer focused. By allowing that person to take real responsibility, the result was that he had felt engaged enough to do something which had a direct effect on the business.

So, the Trust's approach revolved around developing engagement at all levels of the business by creating the environment for people to take responsibility, be creative, and to get on with the job. Managers were trained to understand and see how their behaviour directly affected this environment.

Getting employees to take responsibility

But there was also work with employees. A programme was set up to try to help them understand what the Trust stood for, and therefore to be proud of working there – how it was a good organisation in the sometimes less than scrupulous world of Financial Services. Inviting the Trust's charity clients into the office to explain the work they did helped the Trust's employees understand how they contributed on a much wider scale.

Within the business, training was geared to gain knowledge of other team's work as well as their own. All employees had to study for, and take, a basic pensions exam, even if they were not working in a pensions team.

To reinforce the concept of responsibility, employees increasingly set their own work agenda: work targets and objectives were agreed with managers, and at pay review time it was up to the employees to justify to their managers how engaged and performing they were.

Small, simple activities are often the best. I introduced learning vouchers at the Trust whereby the workforce each received £50 per year to spend on any training – pottery, golf, etc. This cost very little but

- Increased the profile of learning within the business
- Reinforced the message to employees that they were valued

A lot of work was done to help mangers to get their teams to take responsibility at a company wide level. For instance, the business strategy was cascaded to teams and they were asked to produce "contribution statements" – how am I going to add value to the business? These were put in a published "Contribution Statements" for all to see.

Reward engagement in managers and team members

No matter how well the manager serves the team, and no matter how much engagement is at the top of the agenda, the reward package has to be right. I introduced a Total Reward Strategy. This sets out a complete rewards package that includes pay, benefits, culture, learning and development, career development, management style. Many of the components of the reward package depended on how engaged and responsible individuals were.

The whole thing is cemented with a Deal. All employees get this, which says, basically:

"We provide you with great conditions and an environment where you can shine and really contribute. Your side of the Deal is that you must be engaged and perform to your best ability. We will give you extra pay and benefits for being more engaged. We have no place for people who are not engaged."

What are the challenges of this approach?

The team members

Some said they didn't want responsibility. They were happy being directed by their manager. They were comfortable, and didn't want to put themselves out. The Trust's response to this is that it wasn't acceptable. Servant-leadership at the Trust meant the team member took responsibility and got well rewarded for it. Avoiding this responsibility was not an option.

The managers and the business spent a lot of time creating a servant-leadership environment and it's backed up with a Deal and a Total Reward Strategy. If employees don't buy into this approach there's no room for them here. I have to say the vast majority are pretty excited about this approach. They relish the chance to shine.

The managers

More difficult have been the managers. Most like the idea of engaged teams, but getting them to be servant-leaders is much harder. It's about changing a working life of beliefs – all based on the assumption that managers direct. People have, on the whole, spent most of their life being told what to do, and being prevented from taking responsibility. From childhood, school and work, the overriding style tends to be command and control. This is reinforced by management academia and media coverage. Most management qualifications still tell managers they should be controlling, decisive and responsible, and their people skills are still referred to as *"soft"* skills.

The popular TV show, *The Apprentice,* features a manager hiring people who reflect his style, and whose catch phrase is, somewhat aggressively, "You're fired." Against this background, the Trust was asking its managers to delegate responsibility but keep accountability. This is tough. Managers immediately see a potential flaw in this. They are being asked to let their teams have responsibility for things, but if it goes wrong it's the manager who takes the blame.

There's something of a chicken and egg here. Until the managers see the effects of servant-leadership on engaged employees it's hard to persuade them. So, as part of developing the servant-leader approach to engagement, the Trust introduced the concept of 'prior approval'. This is where a manager gives a project to a team member and tells them that no matter what they recommend, the manager will agree.

The Trust rolled this out at both manger and corporate level. So, for example, the Senior Management Team gave a group of volunteer middle managers a communication review project. The senior managers gave prior approval to whatever the group came up with. The results were outstanding.

Another really neat example was with the Trust's stated values. The Trust had always claimed to be values-driven, but no one really knew what those were. I had deliberately avoided listing values and hanging them on walls around the building. Too often I had seen examples of lip service being paid to fashion, but actual behaviour being nothing like the values.

A survey of the workforce showed they wanted written values, so the senior managers agreed that the workforce could themselves decide the values. The workforce was convened in a series of team sessions where they came up with around 30 values statements, which represented the business strategy, and culture of the Trust. All then voted for the top six using the Intranet. This process achieved several goals:

1. The values were bought into by the workforce
2. The engagement message was reinforced
3. Managers saw the effectiveness of 'prior approval' at a corporate level.

At individual level, managers started using 'prior approval' within their teams with really exciting results. The whole concept has proved incredibly powerful at the Trust, with recipients describing feelings of being challenged, engaged, apprehensive, determined and committed.

Trust and humility

These are the two words that have proved the most important in the servant-leadership dictionary at the Trust. If managers don't really trust their teams, how can they be expected to give them responsibility? Managers have to learn humility with the team if the team is going to really trust the manager, and thus cement the engagement relationship.

One of the hardest jobs I faced was enabling this trust between people. I felt that a lot of it was about the manager actually knowing about the team – what the team members' abilities and limits were.

A big learning process for me with 'prior approval' is that the team member must have the ability/knowledge/skills to carry out the work in question. I remember giving a project to one of my HR team to come up with a new employee benefits package. In the spirit of prior approval I said I would agree to whatever she proposed.

When the project came back I realised that is was not acceptable at all, and could not be used. I apologised to the person concerned and tried to work out what had gone wrong.

I realised that you can't get results from servant-leadership unless you ensure that the team members actually have the tools to be able to do the job. The woman I had given the project to did not know how to carry out a benefits review, and so did what she thought was right.

Mistakes happen

But what if the manager delegates responsibility, and it doesn't work out? It's important to understand that servant-leadership at the Trust is not a soft touch. Although the results can be outstanding, it's risky and mistakes do occur. For instance, what if mistakes are made after the manager has given team members the tools and trusted them? I have tried hard to get people into the habit of looking first at the process rather than the person.

Questioning if the process caused the fault first helps to minimise a blame culture at the outset.

However if the mistake was down to an individual, I insist that managers look first to see if the mistake was made in good faith. So the key question is: "Did it happen because there was a genuine attempt by the individual to contribute to the business?"

If so, this tends to be all right with the managers – it's a learning experience. However, if mistakes by individuals are caused by, for example, laziness, negligence or bloody-mindedness, severe sanctions are taken against the individual.

So how is it working?

Eighteen months down the line there have been some fundamental changes to the way things are done at the Trust.

There's a "buzz" amongst the workforce; people talk about engagement, they verify values at all levels, they question others about values. Managers are gradually seeing the benefits of servant-leadership, and the workforce is gradually demanding more responsibility from managers.

The effect on the business has been dramatic. Productivity has risen by around 50% in 12 months. Absence levels and employee turnover are significantly below the industry average. Customer satisfaction surveys show a huge improvement in how the Trust's customers rate the service, and a strong link has been identified between this rating by customers, and the extent to which they refer the Trust to other potential customers.

My view of servant-leadership extends beyond the Trust. The whole process feels good. For instance, getting people to take responsibility at work, helps then take responsibility outside work and in society in general.

Not surprisingly there are some managers and team members who will probably never buy into this style of business, and this includes one or two senior mangers at the Trust. As the drive for short-term results increases, some managers still dismiss people-based strategies as faddish and nebulous – and the more remote Board members can be swayed by these views.

I feel that over time these people are tending to be alienated, and significant pressure is being put on them by their teams to relinquish "macho management". Giving employees responsibility means that they start to demand it.

What we have also tried to do with these managers is to move them into non-people roles. So for instance we have split out pensions administration function into two, one manager to deal with clients (definitely not a servant-leader) and one to deal with the administration teams (very much a servant-leader).

What they learnt

I have four big learning points from the Trust's experience of servant-leadership:

1. You have got to get your CEO, chair or leader into the process, otherwise its very hard to get it to work.

2. Like any culture change, it's hard to get there and dead easy to lose, so be on your guard the whole time.

3. There is no servant-leadership model you can use – each organisation is different and so needs its own approach. You should not try to use it as a management tool.

4. The most important word in the servant-leadership dictionary is 'trust'. Without it any effort expended is wasted.

Why doesn't everyone do it?

To finish this chapter, it is worth asking ourselves, if servant-leadership type cultures are so effective, why isn't everyone doing it?

Why do many (or even most) organisations run on a command and control basis, where bosses tell people what to do, make all the decisions, only let team members do what the job description says, pay them by quantitative targets, and operate ruthless discipline if anyone steps out of line?

The probable reason is that basically it works – these companies are reasonably successful and can be quite profitable.

But what organisation leaders are not realising is that with a little more effort in engaging their people it could work ten times better, and in being ten times more successful, it would enrich the quality of the business, the quality of life of the employees, and in broader terms the quality of life of society in general.

Results of a survey about what engages employees (Towers and Perrin 2004)

Attraction/ recruitment		Retention		Engagement	
Competitive Base Pay	1	Career advancement opportunities	1	Senior managers lead by example in demonstrating the company values	
Work Life Balance	2	Manager inspires enthusiasm for work	2	Employees able to improve skills in the last year	
Career advancement opportunities	3	Provide challenging work	3	Company provides challenging work	
Recognition for work	4	Helping poor performers improve	4	Career advancement opportunities	
Learning and development opportunities	5	Fair and consistent pay determination	5	Employees influence decision making	
Pay rises linked to individual performance	6	Positive overall work environment	6	Company has good reputation as an employer	
Reputation of company as a good employer	7	Intend to work after retirement to stay active	7	Teamwork cares about customer satisfaction	
Competitive benefits	8	Good relationship with works councils	8	Company cares about customer satisfaction	
Variety of work assignments	9	Intend to work after retirement part time in another field	9	Criteria for determining salary levels are fair and consistent	
Level of autonomy in the job	10	If company is successful will share in that success	10	Managers inspire enthusiasm for work.	0
Collaborative work environment	11	Senior management demonstrates values	11	Senior managers have sincere interest in employees well-being	1
Having leading edge technology	12	Senior management interested in employees	12	Employee decision making authority	2
Culture of the company	13	Employees advancement based on performance	13	Positive work environment	3
Customer Focus	14	Appropriate decision-making authority to do the job	14		

6

Servant-Leadership in Local Government

Jane Little

"This is my thesis: caring for persons, the more able and the less able serving each other, is the rock upon which a good society is built. Whereas, until recently, caring was largely person to person, now most of it is mediated through institutions – often large, complex, powerful, impersonal, not always competent, sometimes corrupt. If a better society is to be built, one that is more just and more loving, one that provides greater creative opportunity for its people, then the most open course is to raise both the capacity to serve and the very performance as servant of existing major institutions by new regenerative forces operating within them."

Robert Greenleaf

Why do people enter local government?

It was 20 years ago today...

20 years ago if you asked anyone who came into local government, whether as a councillor or staff, why they'd chosen this path they'd probably say something about "service" – "because it's a public service", "I want to serve my community" or "I believe it's important to be of service in my work." Although there may now be a greater emphasis on performance and targets, "service" is still one of the major drivers for those of us in local and central government.

A job "with the borough"

20 years ago a job "with the borough" was seen as a job for life. Staff working in local government would sacrifice the possibilities of a higher salary in the private sector for the stability and ethos of serving local communities. Local government has changed since then: government targets, performance indicators, financial constraints and boundary changes have led to a more fragmented and performance-driven culture. But I think there is still an underlying wish to work for the public good. This stable background and spirit of service does, I believe, make local government a natural place for exercising servant-leadership.

What is local government anyway?

What we do

There are over two million local government employees in England and Wales, and 21,000 elected councillors (2007 figures). Staff work in organisations big and small, from major county councils to small district councils. They make sure that your rubbish is collected and that your children are educated; that the traffic flows and that builders' scaffolding is safe; that you can use the internet at your local library and that when you buy a litre of petrol a litre is what you get. Then there are the councillors, who spend a lot of time, unpaid, on setting the policies and financial framework for all this (they are not paid a salary, but can claim expenses).

Hierarchies

Is there anything more hierarchical and status-conscious than working in local government? If there is, I'd like to hear about it (or maybe not – it might be too depressing). For the staff, job roles are set and salary levels arrived at according to set grading structures and nationally negotiated pay schemes. There is almost no scope for varying this. "If this is the level of tasks you do, this is the grade for the job and this is what you will be paid." And the councillors get elected, spend time in back-bench roles, then, according to the workings of their party, can gradually progress through minor and major committee appointments, some of them ending up as a committee Chair or as Leader of their party.

"Servant-leadership applies to both designated and situational leaders. Any individual, if they so choose, can provide leadership towards a more caring society".

Robert Greenleaf

Leadership

Local government hierarchies are, I suggest, both a constraint and a freedom when exercising servant-leadership. Where everyone knows everyone else's position in the workplace hierarchy, people naturally look to senior managers to be leaders. So senior managers can use the opportunity to be servant-leaders, and have that ethos accepted because of their role ("this is how I lead"). And those who show leadership qualities (especially servant-leadership) from different places in the organisation have an opportunity to talk about why. The freshness of seeing this happening from an unexpected level gives the opening for conversations about it.

How could servant-leadership be exercised in local government?

"If a good society is to be built, one that is more just and more caring, and where the less able and more able serve one another with unlimited liability, then the best way is to raise the performance of institutions, and sanction natural servants to serve and lead."

Robert Greenleaf

I've worked in local government all my working life and am now in a senior position (in hierarchical terms) and in a position to exercise influence (because of the role I've created). I didn't really think

100

about how I was expressing leadership until I came across servant-leadership a few years ago. Then I started thinking about what I was doing; what I could do, and my influence on those around me. I'm learning about servant-leadership all the time, and it has challenged me to really live its values at work. Here are some things I think can be done to express servant-leadership in local government or similar organisations.

Establish and live by values

Servant-leadership is based on values: the role of the servant-leader in any organisation is surely to understand the business context of the organisation and give a voice to how those values can be expressed in the workplace.

1. If you're a manager, develop values for your team or department and publish them – on the wall, on your intranet, by giving a copy to every member of staff, or whatever works for you. Doing so can be a powerful process that deepens colleagues' understanding of that eternal question: "What are we here for?"
2. If you're not in a situation where you can arrive at team or department values, you can still give expression to your own and make them known. For example, just saying to colleagues, "I believe in helping others as much as I can when at work," can give an opening for creative and eye-opening dialogue.
3. Confront behaviour that is in conflict with your values. Dealing with it will clear the air and re-create stability and trust.

One department I worked with undertook to do this and, after a day of dialogue, drew up the following. Are these servant-leadership values? Not necessarily. But the process of arriving at them (open dialogue, honesty, negotiation) was, I would say, true to servant-leadership principles.

OUR DEPARTMENT'S VALUES AND BEHAVIOURS

We put people first

We always remember that our customers are our business: our services are essential to residents, visitors and workers, and teamwork is essential to deliver them. And we recognise the need to look after ourselves, the service deliverers.

We will always:
- Respect colleagues and customers
- Work together
- Embrace diversity

We will never:
- Assume we know what's best for others
- Undermine or blame people
- Stress people out

We do what we say

We know how important it is to say clearly what we are going to do (and can't do) and why, and then keep our promises. We welcome feedback, and if things go wrong we'll be open about what's happened and do our best to put it right.

We will always:
- Explain clearly what we are doing
- Stick to what we say
- Accept responsibility

We will never:
- Promise what we can't deliver
- Pass the buck
- Brush problems under the carpet

We explore and innovate

Improving our services is based on good ideas, and we value these wherever they come from. We will make the time to explore, try things out, and learn from others.

We will always:
- Push the boundaries
- Keep an open mind
- Learn from experience

We will never:
- Rest on our laurels
- Rule anything out
- Do things that are obviously ridiculous

We are proud of what we do

We believe our services are excellent and that we set the standards for others to follow. We are proud of what we do and the awards we have won.

We will always:
- Aim to be the best
- Welcome challenges
- Celebrate success

We will never:
- Look for reasons not to do things
- Settle for second best
- Give up

Support others and help them grow

One of the key principles of servant-leadership is helping others grow. Robert Greenleaf believed: *"Leaders are first a servant of those they lead. They are a teacher, a source of information and knowledge, and a standard setter, more than a giver of directions and a disciplinarian."* Everyone can do this, whether a manager or not.

- Offer to be a mentor or coach to a colleague, formally or informally. There are people who will value your experience and want to learn from you. Yes, maybe they want it so that they can apply for promotion. Good. Helping someone develop a specific skill or do better in his or her role, not because you have to but selflessly and with love, is the clearest expression of servant-leadership in action.

- Let people move on, with grace. Yes, you may have spent a lot of time with them and feel you've given of yourself, but don't hold them back with chains of obligation. Accept that they will move on and hope that, perhaps, they will spread what they have learned (both skills and ethos) elsewhere.

I think that accepting that people may take what they need and then leave your organisation (and you) is one of the toughest things to accept. We who try to practise servant-leadership in the workplace do give a lot of our heart essence, often against the flow of the organisation's culture, and it's human to want recognition and gratitude in return. But the "chains of obligation" can be a chain on us, too. Letting people go gives us the space to nurture others.

Create the best working atmosphere you can

We spend a lot of time at work, whether actually in the office or carrying out tasks elsewhere. Servant-leaders aim to make the workplace harmonious and creative for everyone. How? There are many simple ways to try:

- Acknowledge people as individuals and make time for conversations. Walk around, say "hello", introduce yourself to people you don't recognise, ask people how they are.

- Make connections and opportunities. Linger in the canteen or coffee area looking friendly and open up conversations with colleagues.

- Make time to listen, whether to work or personal concerns. One of the great needs of our time is for someone to listen to us. Maybe that someone could be you.

- Improve the working environment. Put flowers in the toilets, tidy up the kitchen, clean the office microwave.

One of my greatest successes at work has been putting flowers in the ladies and gents toilets on my floor. It started when the men were complaining about the condition of their loos and I heard (at a servant-leadership conference) that one of the things great companies do is make for a pleasant and creative workplace. Most people don't know it's me who does this. Part of the attraction for me is that our floor has flowers in the toilets and the other 18 floors don't, and there's a bit of a mystery around why…

Challenge the hierarchy and treat people as humans

You are a human being and have equal worth to the Chief Executive and, of course, so do your colleagues. In fact, if you think who makes the workplace a pleasant place to be and who creates a happy environment it probably won't be the Chief Executive; it'll be the guy in the coffee shop, the canteen staff, the receptionists and secretaries.

- Talking to managers and executives as an equal (maybe in the lift or staff canteen) can be refreshing for them. There's no need to lay down the law about how they should be running the place (which might be a challenge too far). However, a simple "how are you?" or comment on your service can open up a dialogue outside the normal hierarchy.

- And, of course, treat all staff in the organisation with respect. Catering staff, cleaners, porters, etc., are probably the lowest-paid in your building. Respecting the work they do and their contribution adds to the "health" of your organisation.

One of the most shining servant-leaders in my workplace is a secretary. She is motivated by her Christian faith, but she doesn't make a show of it. What people notice is that she gives time to others, is always welcoming and helpful, and spreads happiness in her area.

Use your influence for the greater good

Local government can seem like a very bureaucratic, inward-looking place to work. In fact, I believe we underestimate our influence both as colleagues and as policy-makers. Our communities, services and practices are constantly changing and we can contribute to those changes.

- Find out where meaningful conversations take place at work and contribute to them. Many councils have staff surveys, focus groups, sounding boards or other consultation methods. Use them to express your principles with confidence and honesty, and to challenge what needs challenging.

- Most of us in local government work to develop or deliver services direct to local people. That is what we are here for. Reminding ourselves (and perhaps colleagues?) of this and carrying out our role with humility and love is an expression of servant-leadership at its most profound.

Be authentic at work

It seems simple to talk about integrity, honesty, and authenticity. But how often have we hidden our anger, denied our fear or withheld information for our own purposes? The first time you express your feelings it can seem strange or scary; but who can deny or challenge how someone actually feels?

- Say how you feel: in meetings, in conflicts, when you're happy or just any old time.

- Create space for others to do the same and make it safe for them to do so. Just asking people how they feel can touch a part of their being that may not have been brought to work before. But be aware that by doing so you might stir up some feelings that need to be worked through: you may need to learn how to handle this.

One of the best things my organisation has done recently is to subscribe to and publicise an Employee Helpline. This is completely confidential and independent of the council and it gives staff and their immediate families free access to counsellors and advice staff for work or personal problems.

To serve *and* to lead

In hierarchies it's a constant challenge to practise the "serve" element of servant-leadership, perhaps because it goes against the grain of top-down leadership. But sometimes we can get so ingrained in the "serve" that we lose sight of the "lead". Leadership has its place, is very often needed, and can also be a force for good. Think of a great leader and most people name Gandhi, or Nelson Mandela, or Edith Pankhurst – leaders who stood up for what they believed in and challenged the existing power.

Live Servant-Leadership

"Walk the walk", as they say. Keep at it. Do it every day. People will notice and will ask you what motivates you. What a fantastic opportunity to open a conversation about servant-leadership.

Conclusion

There's not much difference between local government and any other large organisation. People work there for various reasons. They do their jobs well or not so well. Fashions in management and leadership come and go and are implemented or maybe just talked about. "Not much difference"... but maybe the difference that does exist – that local government exists to serve local communities – is the area we can draw on for servant-leadership. I believe that the spirit of service is alive and well in local government. All it needs is a bit of nourishment and exposure to the light. We can all help to bring this about.

Recommended reading

James A. Autry, *The Servant-Leader*, Prima

William Bridges, *Managing Transitions: Making the Most of Change*, Nicholas Brealey

Gay Hendricks and Kate Ludeman, *The Corporate Mystic: a Guidebook for Visionaries with Their Feet on the Ground*, Bantam

Judith Leary-Joyce, *Becoming an Employer of Choice*, (CIPD)

Marshall B. Rosenburg, *Nonviolent Communication: a Language for Life*, Puddle Dancer Press

Dave Allan, Matt Kingdon, Kris Murrin and Daz Rudkin, *Sticky Wisdom: How to Start a Creative Revolution at Work*, Capstone

7

Saying Yes, or
The Power of Positive Leading

Jaap Huttenga

"The servant-leader is servant first. It begins with the natural feeling that one wants to serve, to serve first. Then conscious choice brings one to aspire to lead. The difference manifests itself in the care taken by the servant-first to make sure that other people's highest priorities are being served. The best test, and difficult to administer, is: Do those served grow as persons? Do they, while being served, become healthier, wiser, freer, more autonomous, more likely themselves to become servants? And what is the effect on the least privileged in society; will they benefit or, at least, not be further deprived?"

Robert Greenleaf

"Why can't we just say 'Yes' to people?" This sigh was the starting point of one of my highly appreciated conversations with Ralph Lewis. We talked about the way we react to questions and suggestions: interested and inviting, or hesitating and rejecting. We explored all kinds of aspects of "Yes" and "No", especially in relation to leadership and management. It brought us to developing a workshop about 'Saying Yes'. Important elements are reflection and introspection, besides some exercises about acceptance and benevolence. There is also information to pass on. A Dutch CEO of a home for the elderly recently introduced the 'Yes-culture', a thrilling and challenging organisational concept.

108

This chapter is meant to share our enthusiasm with you. It is an invitation to reflect on your own handling "Yes" and "No". Don't expect massive theory, don't fear feathery pep talk. You won't find it here.

50 ways to say "Yes"

Just as, according to Paul Simon, there are fifty ways to leave your lover, there are many ways to say "Yes". In my own Dutch tongue one of the most outspoken ways to reject a proposal is a loud and clear "Yes!" Our attitude and the way we look have to make clear what we really mean. "Yes" and "No" are rarely absolute. For discerning all the different nuances we would need a very detailed scale, and precise instruments. Our reaction is a complicated mix, or even mess, of all kinds of ingredients – emotions, thoughts and afterthoughts, (supposed) knowledge, former experiences, prejudices, the need for keeping up appearances, hidden agendas. These are just a few examples. I may be mistaken, but it seems to me that "Yes" has more nuances than "No". It's really worthwhile to analyse the ingredients of your own Yes-and-no recipe. It helps tracing irrelevant and counterproductive elements in the way you judge questions and situations and to become keen on what really counts.

Nevertheless, in dealing with questions and proposals, mankind seems to be divided in two varieties: those who can't wait to say "Yes" and those who immediately say "No". Let's call them "Yes-ers" and "No-ers". After some thinking the "Yes-ers" often have to acknowledge that "No" would have been a more appropriate answer, whereas the "No-ers" often see some possibilities after all. But anyhow, we all seem to have our own primary or spontaneous reaction. (Probably the most common answer is "Well...", but this can hardly be considered to be a spontaneous answer. It often is a sadder and wiser reaction after former misjudgements.) What about you? Are you a "Yes-er" or a "No-er"? And the people you're living or working with? Maybe the difference on this point is the main reason why somebody irritates you all the time. What makes us react the way we do?

"No" seems more natural than "Yes"

It is hard to know what configures our immediate and spontaneous reactions. All kinds of scientists offer us a variety of reasons why saying "No" is our most natural reaction in unexpected situations. Reality is experienced as a threatening chaos. It demands quite a lot of basic trust to live open-minded and to consider the unexpected as challenging instead of threatening. It is hard to survey all possible aspects of a situation in our complex society and culture. Often an important part of bringing up children is teaching them to be careful. "No" is a very common word in the world of raising children. We have learned to take "No" as a firm starting point in dealing with questions. Many sincere wishes of children are immediately and automatically rejected with a simple "No", only to be followed with "because I say so". Somebody once said that raising children is nothing but breaking their will. Bringing up children this way does not stimulate them to become self-confident, creative and daring, but prepares them for living in a cage of safe and secure correctness. Regarding this it really is a miracle that there are so many positive feeling, thinking and acting people.

Anyhow, our spontaneous reaction is related to a fundamental attitude towards life. During the years, however, we are all conditioned, mostly in the sense that we constantly want to create security. This may lead to reactions that are contradictory to our fundamental attitude. Feeling insecure in your relationships, feeling guilty about saying "No" can lead to pleasing somebody by saying "Yes", even if it is not in accordance with your will or understanding. Many people, on the other hand, have learned to create a negative, rejecting attitude, because they were told again and again that being kind and positive is the silliest thing to do. When you want to become a "Yes-er" you should start with accepting yourself as you are, and the people around you as they are. That's where it all begins, and at the same time it is the hardest part of the road.

Some common, but weird ideas about saying "No"

However natural this all may seem to be, we may expect leaders to know themselves well enough to be aware of the psychological and spiritual aspects of their character and behaviour. These aspects have an enormous impact on the way they are leading. In his wonderful essay J. Parker Palmer wrote about the shadows inside a lot of leaders.[22] He mentions:

- Deep insecurity about their own identity, their own worth
- The perception that the universe is essentially hostile to human interest
- 'Functional atheism' – the belief that ultimate responsibility for everything rests with me: "If nobody does it, I will..."
- Fear of the natural chaos of life, leading to the need of order and control and the abandoning of dissent, innovation, challenge and change.
- The denial of death, which makes us maintain things that are no longer alive or maybe never have been.

Sadly enough, management and organisations are often furnished in a "No" style. Where power and control are considered to be the keywords of management, the frequent use of "No" is inevitable. People with a fearful mindset always seemed to be most suitable to become a manager. They found support in a lot of presumptions about "Yes" and "No".

"If I say 'Yes' to you I cannot say 'No' to somebody else"

It is quite easy to unmask this myth. Just put it the other way around and it is clear how ridiculous it is: "If I say 'No' to you I cannot say 'Yes' to somebody else." If somebody legitimates his negative reaction this way he shows that he is not willing or daring to make his own decisions. Maybe he is not even capable of doing so. At least

---

[22] J. Parker Palmer, 'Leading From Within', in *Insights On Leadership*, Larry C. Spears (ed), John Wiley & Sons Inc, 1998

he refuses to be accountable. Leadership means to be able to see people and situations as they are, without generalising them. People have the right to be treated that way. Most of them accept a negative answer if it is well substantiated and applicable to the situation. A weighted "No" is acceptable when, in another situation, a weighted "Yes" can be expected. To be honest, I'm convinced that believing this myth of the precedent is a sign of bad leadership. If you really want to defend your decisions with a precedent you should try this one: We always judge questions or situations on their own.

Saying "No" is cheaper

Whoever thinks saying "No" is cheaper than saying "Yes" probably doesn't take all the costs into account. It can be compared with calculating the costs of a production process without regarding the costs of environmental damage. Companies still come away with this, but today a lot of them find procedures for environmentally neutral production, for example, by planting a tree for travelling by airplane. Even if this can be seen only as window-dressing, it shows a growing awareness of a broader spectrum of costs.

Saying "No" often produces opposition and objections. You need far more time to explain and defend your "No" than a "Yes". Nobody asks "Why?" when he gets "Yes" for an answer, where "Why not?" is the logical and legitimate reaction to the rejection of a wish or proposal. Opposition often goes underground, and does his devastating work like a peat moor fire. When objections grow into official complaints and procedures it is very hard to calculate the costs in time and money. Saying "No" demotivates, and erodes commitment. That, too, has to be calculated as a cost of saying "No"! On the other hand, you have to regard the profits of saying "Yes". People feel themselves respected. Do as you would be done by; benevolence is a mutual process. Managers who strictly hold to the rules – for example, in case of a leave of absence because of the death of beloved one – make their employees claim the utmost, where others who give carte blanche see their co-workers return even before their leave has ended.

Saying "Yes" is an invitation to creativity. New products or better procedures are only developed in an atmosphere that stimulates the pleasure of experiments and discoveries, including the risk of failure. So be aware of the costs of saying "No" and what you gain by saying, "Yes" and you will never again think that saying "No" is cheaper. (Just for fun you should try to describe the successive steps in a process that arises from a blunt "No". Subsequently calculate the direct and consequential costs. You will be amazed.)

Saying "No" is easier

Maybe this is true, but only for the time being, just as saying "Yes" is often a short-term solution to a problem. I have already mentioned all the extra work to be done and the resistance to be overcome. When saying "No" is your basic and general attitude, you must be prepared to have power without the indispensable authority to establish it, to make it accepted and fruitful. This kind of power is not easy to maintain, but very hard! Saying "No" produces a feeling of being in control, but the opposite is more likely: emphasising your power to control is an invitation to undermine it.

And what is the result of all that controlling? Isabel Lopez, a regular speaker at servant-leadership conferences, once told a story from her childhood, about her grandmother baking cookies for Christmas. As soon as the first tray was taken out of the oven Isabel's younger brother tried to grab some of the crisp and warm cookies. She managed to keep him out of the kitchen and away from the cookies all day. Finally, when all the work was done, he was allowed to eat one. It was rock hard and tasted awful. It seemed that they had in fact been using salt instead of sugar all day! Had the youngster been allowed a taste from the first batch – had Isabel said "Yes" – then only that first batch of cookies would have been inedible, and the day would not have been wasted.

Saying "No" is powerful

Saying "No" is far more often associated with power than "Yes". "No" seems to be a firm statement, while "Yes" is often seen as soft or indifferent. In many situations, however, saying "Yes" calls for a lot more courage than saying "No". In many situations the intention of saying "No" is to keep the situation as it is. Rightly or wrongly, "No" feels saver and more secure than "Yes". For "Yes" you need the courage to be open to change, the perseverance to resist all the "No's" around you, the creativity to find solutions, and the power to realise them. So, saying "Yes"asks for a quite strong character and personality.

So it's better to say "Yes"

When you consider all this you have to acknowledge that saying "No" has hardly any positive effect. Often it is really counterproductive. Saying "No" kills motivation and commitment, obstructs creativity and the development of new concept, and diminishes self-esteem and the joy of working with your talents. "No" creates separation instead of cooperation. "No" has to do with control, "Yes" with trust. Saying "Yes" creates a challenging situation, where everybody likes to do one's best and to contribute one's talents and dedication. The benefits of saying "Yes" are obvious, when you are prepared to see them.

So if you are born or raised as a "Yes-er" there is no reason for changing your fundamental attitude. Of course, it isn't that simple. Everybody is interlaced in many systems and networks where power and authority play an important role. Even if you want to lead in a positive way, a higher level in the hierarchy can prohibit that by bombarding you with loads of "No's". You can see yourself as the Lone Ranger, called to save the world in general or at least your own company, but it is very hard to stand alone. To be positive and to be able to act that way you need a receptive atmosphere. Well, at least you can try to make a start.

Loving chaos

One of the main conditions for being a "Yes-er" is to love chaos, or at least not to be afraid of it. You must be able to handle the unexpected. You need the flexibility to deal with continuously changing plans and situations. You need a helicopter view to oversee everything, and at the same time the perspective of a frog to be aware of the details. And you need great dreams, ideals and concepts, which happens to be one of the characteristics of servant-leadership. In his already mentioned essay J. Parker Palmer writes: 'The insight we forget from our spiritual traditions is that chaos is the precondition to creativity. Any organisation (or any individual) that does not have a safe arena for creative chaos is already half dead. When a leader is so fearful of chaos as not to be able to protect and nurture that arena for other people, there is deep trouble.'

As somebody else said, saying "No" is an automatism. "No" is an absolute creativity killer. A manager must have the guts to create chaos; on the edge of chaos creativity gets a chance.

The 'Yes-culture' of Hans Becker

Earlier I quoted Hans Becker, the CEO of the umbrella-organisation Humanitas, with 28 homes, 6000 elderly people and 2300 personnel. In the Netherlands he became famous with the development of a 'Yes-culture'. In his organisation the answer to every sincere question or proposal, whether it comes from residents or staff, is "Yes". Colleagues are afraid to follow him. There is always too little money for care. How can you control your budget if you deliver yourself to unpredictable wishes and desires? Becker, however, proves to be one of the few managing directors in the care sector who has no financial problems. A 'Yes-culture' is cheaper than a 'No-culture'!

The fundamental positive attitude towards personal needs and wishes creates a pleasant and beneficial atmosphere. It is a way of living and working together. Residents are not only patients, employees are far more than simply efficient working people, and visitors are not regarded as inconvenient, disturbing the daily schedule. All together they are seen as the people who form a community, each of them with their own contributions and gifts, needs and desires. A community where everybody can feel at home. Normally, visitors come only to see one of the patients, and after visiting hours they leave as soon as possible. But what if they can feel themselves as 'one of us', temporarily taking part in the daily life of the small society of a home, with facilities specially created for them? It's obvious that they become committed and involved, willing to lend a hand. A community is a mutual, multidimensional interest, instead of a one-way relationship. Comparatively the same can be said of residents and staff.

Of course, not everything is possible. This 'Yes-culture' includes the obligation to consider all possible solutions before saying "No". If that is the case, the negative outcome has to be explained carefully. But starting with the intention to make things possible, lots of creativity and inventiveness are released, and the pleasure of solving puzzles gets a chance. Often proposals and requests surprisingly create more efficient or less expensive solutions. You just have to be openly receptive to the unexpected. In many homes, for example, pets are not allowed. But I have been told, "Pets turn out to be a lot cheaper than all kinds of therapists. Animals often give more distraction than our expensive staff can do. So it is possible to make time to do other things." Of course, not everything works out well, but the 10% of failures don't equal the 90% of successful solutions. And at least you have been through a lot of fun.

Four basic values of 'Humanitas'

This 'Yes-culture' is one of the four basic values of Humanitas, the umbrella organisation Becker works for. The other three are: Direction of your own life, Use it or lose it and Organisation as an extended Family. Of course, the social service sector differs in many ways from business and industry. For example, not only do you have to deal with personnel, but also with residents. However, the presumption that a culture like this is not fit for the profit economy is all too easy. You just have to transfer it to your own situation. The invested time and creativity will prove to be worthwhile.

Direction of your own life

One of the consequences of moving to a home for elderly people is giving up your independence. People who will have successfully managed their own responsibilities for such a long time are suddenly regarded as helpless and in need of guidance and care. They are submitted to house rules and rhythms. A woman in a wheelchair once said to me: "You always have to beware that they don't take you to wherever you don't want to be." Of course there can be a good reason for taking over the direction of somebody's life, but in most of the cases only for a part of it.

It is the same with working people. Employees don't have to be led by the nose. In many situations they themselves are the best experts, and know what to do or how to solve a problem. There is a lot of satisfaction to be found in taking responsibility for your own work. Alas, many managers are convinced of the need to control everything (a symptom of uncertainty) and doing so implicitly shows their lack of trust in their co-workers. And it changes many employees into minimalists: why should I do more than I am asked for? Hierarchy and leading are necessary and useful, but only as far as the ones who are being led request them.

Use it or lose it

People in care centres are often seen and treated as 'flat characters'. Just one aspect of their being seems to be relevant: they need care. Their talents and capacities are no longer used and respected. It's a great loss, first of all for the people involved. A main part of their way of being and raison d'être is put aside. Doing things creates the feeling of being useful. It gives reason to be involved in society, to take part in all kinds of developments, and to keep developing oneself. Activity brings social contacts and all kinds of subjects to think and talk about. Besides the relief of being cared for, there is often the frustration about not being taken seriously any more. No wonder many cared-for people consequently withdraw or isolate themselves. All kinds of activities have to be organised to keep them moving.

117

It is also a great loss for the organisation they are living in. Why spoil all the skills and experience of so many people? You can have them for free! The fear of asking too much from these people should not lead to the conclusion of not asking them anything at all.

You don't need much imagination to see the similarities with the working place. Many employees are only hired for one task. They are not expected to interfere with other elements of the company, or even the (production) processes they are involved in. Here you have an important cause of burnout. Many workers see things going wrong (or less successfully) while having the insight or experience to solve the problem. Just because they are not in the right position, they have no 'right' to act.

It's embarrassing to see how many people, forced to exploiting only one of their capacities at work, need other activities to experience satisfaction! Everybody has far more resources than the simple work they are doing. Use them or lose them.

Extended family

Larry Spears, former CEO of the Greenleaf Center in the USA suggested a formula for building societies through the 'ten characteristics of the servant-leader'. Human beings are social creatures, living in groups and communities. We don't live in small villages anymore, but in a global society. Many relationships are reduced to functional contacts. Even care, pre-eminently a multi-dimensional relation between people, has become more and more a matter of technical action. Hospitals and nursing homes reflect these developments, and have become sterile buildings. It's the same with companies and factories. In many situations, daily work is nothing but a productive activity instead of sharing work, ideals, and social life with each other.

People are longing for societies and communities again. A working place can be such a community. We know of many companies organised as families in the beginning of the 20th century. Ford in the USA, Bata in the Czech Republic, and Philips in the Netherlands are well-known examples. After some time this organisational model disappeared again; maybe it wasn't modernistic anymore. Of course, one of the problems was the quite paternalistic atmosphere. Nowadays we can try to rebuild working places as social communities, but leave out the paternalistic 'paterfamilias'.

One of the conditions is to reshape the culture in the organisation, and give more room for social contacts. But that is not enough. Our buildings need a makeover to facilitate other activities for the workers and possibly as well for the neighbourhood where a company is located. Extended families need a 'real' home.

Yes-culture

A 'Yes-culture' really has to be a culture. It has to be supported by the whole community in an organisation. Of course, a good structure is necessary, but structure follows culture. Often ideas like these are just the hobby of the person in charge. The only result will be disappointment and reinforcement of old, familiar and proven prejudices: "They only do it for the money. They only want to gain profit from my kindness." A 'Yes-culture' is to a great extent dependent on mutuality.

"Yes" cannot be unconditional. The basic and primary intention is to enable things to be in line with the goal and mission of an organisation. The conditions must be related to the subject itself and not to all kind of hidden needs or agendas..

For most people a reasonable "No" is acceptable if at the same time a reasonable "Yes" is not withheld. A positive atmosphere doesn't mean there isn't place for a "No" anymore. But everybody remembers situations where parents rightly or wrongly said "No". Everybody is aware of the experience of a kind of balance between the two.

A 'Yes-culture' is a welcoming, inviting culture. You feel yourself free to take part in it. The effect of such a culture is hard to overestimate. It affects all aspects of living and working together. It takes a lot time and effort to make it work, but you will enjoy it. You need to be a pro-active person to establish and nurture such a culture. But maybe it is even better to be 'pre-active', always asking, 'What can I do for you?

What's it going to be? Yes or No?

In many cases changing from "No" to "Yes" is just a matter of analysing and rethinking. Instead of focusing on the objections, we should look for the possibilities. Many threats are only threats because we are trained to see them that way. In fact, they can be excellent opportunities. In their race against each other, "Yes" always starts with the heavy handicap of disbelief and hesitation where "No" has no burden at all, not even the obligation to prove itself. We can consider it as a sign of how powerful "Yes" really is – in horse racing you only get handicapped when you are too strong for the other competitors.

In fact it is the race between freedom and security, two issues which usually, but mistakenly are mixed up. Do we really need so much security that we accept the loss of our freedom?

8

Hostmanship and Servant-Leadership

Jan Gunnarsson and Olle Blohm

Introduction

Hostmanship, the art of making people feel welcome, was introduced as a practical philosophy in Scandinavia in 2002. While first having a focus on how to meet people as guests, we looked for a leadership approach that would enable the creation of hostmanship in organisations and places. After some searching we came in contact with The Robert Greenleaf Centre for Servant-Leadership, and found what we were looking for.

A welcoming world

We long for a world of true joy and meaning in our lives, where we live in true community and all humans feel expected and welcome. We call our dream "A Welcoming World".

Imagine a world where everybody is equally welcome. This sounds like a dream, we know, but many of us share this dream today. A world where we bring forth the best in ourselves, where our talents and personalities are cherished, where we are free to meet each other as the human beings we are, and to see that which unites us instead of seeing that which divides us. One could say that it has taken life close to 14 billion years to evolve to a point where it is, through us, able to reflect on creation itself. This leaves us with an important choice: to see the world as a candy store to exploit, or as something in our trust.

We need to define our role. To succeed as humans, we cannot look upon ourselves only as guests here on earth, but rather as its hosts – hosts who practise hostmanship, the art of welcoming, based on six fundamentals: serving others, perceiving wholeness, practicing dialogue, taking responsibility, expressing consideration and searching knowledge.

Let's take a look at each of them in turn:

Serving

We use our talents and experiences to the benefit of something larger, or someone else. We meet each human being with thoughts of how we can make life easier for them. We recognise that all our actions are meant to serve those around us, and that our places serve the people who live and work there, plus all those who have chosen to visit them today and tomorrow.

Serving someone else is an often misunderstood art in the times we live in. We have begun to believe that service is the same thing as voluntarily acting as a doormat. Let us now reclaim the word, and return to it its proper meaning. To serve is to be there for someone else. To ask oneself: "What can I do to make you feel better?" A characteristic of the serving organisation is that it has a serving leadership. Leaders who serve their employees – where they primarily care about the world and daily life of their employees.

Serving is the foundation for finding true meaning in life.

Wholeness

We see and we understand the larger context. We need to understand and feel in our heart that "a pain in one is pain in all, and progress for you is progress for me". We need to understand that a person we meet is something much greater than what meets our eyes. And we need a perspective that does not only include us as a person, the organisation we work for, our community, nation or region, but one that sees us first and foremost as global citizens and even vehicles of life itself.

Dialogue

We seek understanding and agreement. We listen not only to words, but also to the entire person, and we dare to open ourselves up to diversity. We receive critique as the gift it is, and are thankful for the confidence by ignoring pre-conceived notions. We use our courage to understand all aspects of a problem.

In order to be able to carry on a dialogue, we must first learn to listen. We human beings cling tightly to our deep-rooted patterns and pre-conceived notions. We always believe that one plus one is two, and often answer before we hear the end of the question. There are three ways to meet a person when a problem occurs. One, we can enter into a debate and explain that the other party is wrong. Two, we can choose a discussion and convince her that we are right. Or three, we can listen and try to understand the context while beginning a dialogue. Opening up to a dialogue at each meeting means taking everybody seriously. By being able to think together we will find solutions not reachable by an individual person or culture.

Responsibility

We take responsibility for our actions, which means that we stand by our ways to react and relate to all that happens to us. We take responsibility for the world that is ours, and we dare meeting people with our entire essence, without blaming circumstances, our history, or other people.

Taking responsibility means using our courage. It is unrealistic to feel responsible for all that happens in the world; on the other hand, we always take responsibility for how we choose to react to what happens. We may choose between taking the matter seriously and blaming someone else. We may choose to learn something, or to walk away unaffected. Taking responsibility is a question of solidarity, putting ourselves on the side of the other party and helping to improve the world we live in. A choice perhaps not always appreciated by our organisation, but which in the end creates stronger relationships and more responsible individuals.

Consideration

We dare to use our hearts and we search for the human being inside ourselves and see the human being in others. We trust our friendly instincts regardless of whom we meet or where the meeting takes place.

Caring is the heart of hostmanship. An empathetic, considerate person easily becomes a good host. For such a person, it seems natural to take care of others and to look out for someone's best interests. Therefore, it's easy to release the human in ourselves and to meet all others first of all as fellow human beings. A caring system never forgets whom the system serves, and that this recipient most likely will act just as human beings usually act. To let consideration rule in an activity is seeing the human side in those who seek us out. Being caring also involves our use of resources, the environment, and how we cherish our own and other people's time and money.

Knowledge

We meet human beings where they are and understand that which they understand. We gratefully and humbly carry our knowledge and serve when we use it. We open up to all cultures and people, regardless of background. Good knowledge is a given when it comes to hostmanship. We know what we do and why we do it.

But, having knowledge is something far greater than this. Utilising hostmanship is also building a culture where we constantly learn things that enrich our experiences. This applies as much to a personal hostmanship as to an activity. A culture where each question is taken seriously, and where the important thing is not always the answer, but who asks the question. For a global citizen who will take responsibility for the whole, science and the understanding of man and nature is paramount.

There they are, six fundamentals, not a whole religion, no paragraphs and no exceptions, just six ordinary words that cannot be misunderstood. And we express them in three different stages. First is "welcoming others", as strangers, customers, etc. Then comes "welcoming each other" as family, neighbours, colleagues and partners. Finally – and the core of hostmanship – is "welcoming oneself".

The creation of a welcoming world demands a different view of our relationship to life. We need to be a "homo hospes", a welcoming human, whose consciousness has evolved to a level where a welcoming world is possible. "Homo hospes" is a human being that defines richness not by how much one accumulates but by how much one gives. Also, we must not try to implement our way of life in every corner of the world, but rather help others from where they are to reach a point where they can create their unique way.

Hostmanship demands no religion, no diploma, no party politics and no passport. We only need humans who have regained their compassion and sense of humanity. We need storytellers who want to tell the story to as many as possible. Success is counted by the number of people who have been inspired by it, and are enabled to play their part in creating a more welcoming world. We need to tell our story in schools, institutions and everywhere people gather. We need to tell it to children, adults, leaders, politicians and others. Because, our story is not something completed that should be implemented, it's a conversation, a journey where the road is created by many different footsteps.

Mankind and all life on planet Earth are at this moment in time facing unprecedented challenges and possibilities. By understanding that we all are part of the same tribe on a common journey, we will thrive and be able to stand with dignity before life and generations to come.

Manager or leader

Since you are reading this book, I assume you see yourself as a leader. Let's assume that you have found your way and know who you are, what you want and why. You enjoy the responsibility you have and want more in life than power over others.

OK, the next question is: Do you want to be a manager or a leader?

The most obvious difference is that a manager is appointed from above and a leader from below. A leader is someone you follow, as well as a person who can handle having followers. A leader has the ability to build enthusiasm in the people around him and thrives in the role at the top, while knowing that he doesn't have all the answers.

I will readily admit that for many people there is a conflict between being a complete person and leading others. There are those who see their ascendancy to the corner office as a shortcut to all the answers. Their appointment is final proof they have made the grade. Of course, that's not the case. After a few months the questions return and they continue to search. And if they ever happen to find themselves, they may have already lost their fire.

Those who seem to do best and thrive in the role usually never seek it out. They have developed their thoughts and ideas, and as others have come to share them they have taken on a leadership position. In other words, their goal has been to see how far their ideas would take them, not necessarily to find others who agree with them.

A true leader is responsible for his own life. This may seem obvious, but unfortunately it is not. It sometimes seems more difficult to lead yourself than to lead others. Many of the business crises in the last decade happened because managers lost their sense of themselves and became inebriated with the notion of leadership. Basically they no longer knew where they belonged. Were they one of us mere mortals or something greater? Rather than make fun of their shortcomings, I would ask whether these gentlemen were all that unusual in losing their footing. Can anyone suffer the same indignity? Of course. I would dare to say it's fairly common. When your job consumes a large chunk of your time and the accolades pile up, it is easy to forget why you are where you are and who you were in the beginning. All your love is soon directed at the person who looks at you in the mirror in the morning.

There is a picture stuck in my mind of the Rolling Stones making their entrance on the stage of Ullevi Arena in Göteborg on their 'Bridges to Babylon' tour. They crossed an artificial bridge rising above the audience. I usually think that once you have crossed that bridge, metaphorically, it is hard to come back down to earth. (Imagine it yourself. Close your eyes and cross that bridge while more than ten thousand people stomp their feet and scream your name.) The hard part is that you must be willing to be followed while understanding that people are not following you, but your ideas. The fire, energy and passion you have as a person have to rub off. Take away these qualities and you are left naked, no different from the rest of us.

A leader's essence, his thoughts and passion, are like a work of art. Imagine it as a fantastic book. When we talk about an author, we mean the creator of a work we love. We love the book, so we pay tribute to its author. One person who understood this was Jean-Paul Sartre, who refused the Nobel Prize. He knew it would only draw unwanted attention to him as a person rather than the works he had created. He claimed he'd already been richly rewarded by the mere fact that he had written his books. This quality is hard to find today. We expect our leaders to personify their organisations, and have a vision they burn for, but society has a tendency to reduce this to little more than a face in a photo. And if the camera happens to find your face attractive, charming or otherwise appealing, you run a big risk of becoming something other than what made you a success in the first place.

Manager or leader, that is the question. If you are regarded as the latter, you can expect special demands, but don't let that slow you down. It is your personality, your ideas and your fire we want to light our way. Not your vanity.

Spreading success

I was once contacted by an athletic shoe manufacturer who told me, "We advertise everywhere for millions, attract people's interest and get them in the stores. But once they're there, they buy our competitor's brand. Do you think better hostmanship would get them to choose our shoes – the ones they saw in the ad?"

"No," I said. "But you might think about selling rowing

machines."

"Rowing machines?"

"Yes. That's how it works. I see an ad and it reminds me I need to exercise. So I go to the store to buy a new pair of shoes. But with good hostmanship, I'd probably walk out of there with a rowing machine instead."

He looked puzzled and asked what I meant.

"Good shoes are important to have," I said. "Everyone knows that – at least if you plan to do any running. The connection is obvious. The problem is what comes after I've made the connection between new shoes and running. That's when a little voice asks me, 'Is it that time of year again?'

'Yes, it's about time,' I reply, grabbing my midsection with two hands. 'I've got to work on this.'

'How'd it go last time?'

'Well, not so good.'

'It's a lotta work, and then we had that rainy period and you kind of lost a step.'

'Yeah, something like that.'

'That's the way it usually goes. Fall came so quickly last year, didn't it? It got dark and cold. You like running?'

'Like and like … what are you gonna do? But this morning I saw an ad for a nice pair of shoes and it struck me that it's time to get going again.'

'Have you ever thought about a rowing machine instead? If you really want to get rid of that thing. Come over here. You can fold it up and stick it under your bed. Take it out in the morning and row for fifteen minutes while you listen to the radio or watch TV.'

"So you see, better hostmanship probably wouldn't help you sell more shoes, but it might help people to meet their goals and lose weight."

Anyone who seeks success should learn to ask "why?" rather than "what?" I never cease to be amazed by people who constantly ask others what they are doing, what their budget is, what they are planning to do next. These questions are totally pointless, and the person asking isn't going to be helped by the answers. If they instead asked why they had chosen to do what they're doing or how they plan to find new guests, the answers are worth considering.

This probably applies to your organisation as well. Most companies I know live in a "what" world. They can fairly easily answer the question, "What are your guests buying?" But they usually have little to say when you ask, "Why do they buy it?"

Hostmanship is all about spreading success. Helping those you come into contact with take the decisive step from satisfied to successful. It's about looking at that other person and figuring out the real reason why you are interacting at that moment. This is true whether you are speaking to your staff or to someone who has approached your company. In many cases you are talking to a messenger, who will spread success to others. You also have to understand the situation and consider the next step in the chain. Focusing entirely on those in front of you is like opening up a fancy ice-cream parlour on the beach and selling only two flavours: rum raisin and tiramisu. You probably won't do well. Down by the beach most of your customers are more interested in satisfying the little tyke who doesn't quite reach up to your counter and just wants a vanilla popsicle.

The word "successful" is interpreted differently by different people. It is too often associated with money and position. To me, a person achieves success when his needs are satisfactorily met – when he finds meaning in what he does, even if he cannot always express what those needs are. This is why it's important to understand what other people's real needs are – to anticipate when they will approach you, and understand what they are thinking when they do. You also have to be aware of the connections the human brain makes – how life sometimes makes us feel like we are stuck in a giant shopping mall, where the stores are lined up in an endless succession and all the colours and greetings blend together. We get confused, wander off in one direction or another and get stuck in the wrong stores.

If you are concerned only with your products, if you are convinced you sell the coolest, best-looking shoes in the world and that it's inconceivable everyone doesn't realise it, you will sell a lot of shoes that end up in the back of people's closets. Or if you look at your town and say, "Isn't it beautiful here? If only more people moved here, they'd see how fantastic it is." Or if you run a hardware store and believe that everyone dreams about drills and new tools? If that's the case, the best you can expect is satisfied customers. As long as you see the world from this perspective, you will never maximise your sales. The point is to stop obsessing about your products and services and instead begin meeting needs. People are coming to you to get rid of a flabby stomach, because they're lonely and want to socialise by joining the local softball team, to live closer to someone they like, to take a job they are trained for or to find a hook for the hand towel in their bathroom.

For many people, this is a revelation. A bank manager on the island of Åland in the Baltic Sea came up to me after a seminar and said, "I always thought I lent money, when what I was really doing was helping businesses to realise their missions or people to fulfil their dream of a beautiful home." That's it exactly. It's certainly not the debt they want.

Another example of how easy it is to obsess about a product is to go into a bar and order a non-alcoholic beer. Maybe you're driving, but you want to sit there with your friends and have a beer. Your ultimate need isn't the beer but being part of the gang. You are usually told it is only available in the bottle. But what if you want a pint, like your friends? While it's understandable the bar may not have non-alcoholic beer on tap, it's also strange that no-one offers to open up two bottles and pour them into a mug. Even if there is a little left over, who cares? What does a sip or two of non-alcoholic beer cost anyway? A few cents? This is an example I often use when I am speaking to groups. And you should have seen what happened when I used it with an audience from the restaurant industry.

I told the story the way I usually do and said I was surprised no one ever offered to serve me non-alcoholic beer in a mug. A discussion broke out. It began as expected: "We only serve non-alcoholic beer by the bottle."

"Yes, I know," I said. "But you have mugs, don't you?"

"Then I'd have to open up two bottles, wouldn't I?"

"Yes, exactly."

"That's going to be an expensive beer. More expensive than a regular draft."

"Then I don't want it. What do you charge for a large draft?"

"Forty-four."

"OK," I said. "Let's say that a bottle of non-alcoholic beer costs twenty-five kronor and that you charge ten kronor for the second bottle. Then my beer would cost me thirty-five kronor. That would be fair, wouldn't it? If you're only paying one krona per bottle, you've still earned nine kronor on the second bottle and probably still have half left. And I've gotten exactly what I wanted."

"You can't do it like that. We can't charge for half a bottle."

"Why not? I want a pint of beer. Do you seriously mean that's impossible?"

"Yeah ... or, no ... of course, but ..."

"But?"

"Well, I'm not allowed to. I can't just charge whatever I like. We're using up two bottles."

"Yes, if you pour out what's left of the second one, you will be. I know that. But you're also making a profit and meeting the needs of your guest."

"It doesn't work like that at our restaurant," one guy said suddenly. "She comes at night and counts all the bottles. If the number is wrong, I have to make up the difference."

"I see. 'She' does it."

That put an end to the discussion.

The restaurateurs in the front row seemed to realise what a predicament they were in and shook their heads. A couple of them came up to me after the seminar in disbelief.

"That was the worst argument I have ever heard," one said.

"Yeah, think about all the mistakes we make."

The trick, of course, is to see that a need exists before anyone points it out. It is fascinating to think that this kind of analysis often affects an organisation so deeply that it has to rewrite its mission statement. At the same time you have to remember not to mix up form and function, and to keep a clear picture of the company's vision and why it is in business. Many companies have changed the

131

way they do business in recent years due to new technology. In doing so, they have retained their form but changed their function. Like the video game company that one night suddenly shut down all its offices after realising it could serve customers better by making its games available on the Internet. The goal wasn't to have a bunch of stores. It just wanted people to buy their games and play them. But it is hard sometimes. I have personally sat through countless meetings and discussed changes that have confused form and function. Where old, ingrained ideas about function have stopped people from doing the same thing in a new, more effective way.

You have to stop obsessing about your product and take a better look at the people you serve. Look at things from their perspective. See the world from their vantage point instead of trying to do what's "normal." Meet each person with your eyes wide open. Discover subtleties and be willing to accept change and adapt to it.

Thinking about needs affects product development and how you sell your products. But that's just the beginning. As a welcoming leader, your goal is to get your employees to blossom. You also want to be in touch with their search for meaning. You want to see what drives them – to see them dream, dare, believe and do. You have to understand what they want out of life and make decisions on that basis. It might even mean promoting or dismissing those who have reached their goals. "Congratulations," you could say. "You're done here. You can go now." So we can instead concentrate on those who haven't figured it all out yet.

To spread success to his employees, a leader must think first as a person. Some people need more support than others, and a welcoming leader therefore adapts his leadership to the situation at hand. There are plenty of emotions in a workplace, and a leader has to identify the driving forces moving his people. This usually requires an ongoing dialogue rather than an annual review, when each employee's needs are expected to be neatly packaged and handed over to the leader. It is more a question of the leader acting like a coach and offering himself as a mirror so that employees can discover themselves. In this way, a welcoming leader helps his employees find their own ways to success. The road is clear if the leader pays attention, is considerate and keeps his eyes open. Sit down with your employees. Ask questions that will encourage them to tell you about themselves, what they are thinking and how they feel.

It is also important to connect your employees' search for meaning with the company. All of us have to go a step further and offer a workplace that asks itself what it is, what it wants and why. It is becoming less and less sustainable to just sell a product, whatever it may be, unless your employees feel it offers benefits and meets a true need.

One way to go about it is to follow the example of Medtronic, which makes pacemakers. Every Christmas, it invites in patients who have received a pacemaker to talk about their lives and express their gratitude to the staff for being alive.

9

Servant-Leadership in South Africa

Lance Bloch

The grizzled soldier of Umkhonto we Sizwe (armed force of the 'liberation army' of the ANC) held up a match to the group, lit it, and said: "This match represents the fire that burned within me, for freedom and justice for my people. But those flames also burned me, consumed me with anger and bitterness towards the government, and whites in general. But, that time is over. I want to build this new South Africa together. Recognise that I am a human like you, and we can go forward together, build a country for all of us." This moving scene happened at one of the first groups I facilitated to help integrate the armies of the ANC and the South African government. This was in early 1994, even before the landmark democratic elections in April. I knew then that – contrary to some expectations of a bloodbath – the "Rainbow Nation" was not just a dream, an illusion, but could become a reality. I saw previous enemies, who had been ready to kill each other on sight, often become firm friends.

Fast forward to May 8-9, 2002. I had gained a huge amount of experience since then in my own training and development company, Lance Bloch & Associates, in the areas of change and transformation in general – working in the areas of diversity, change management, leadership development, emotional intelligence, and what I call "Building Workplace Community", which I consider to be an advance on Team Building. I was invited to be one of the keynote presenters at the inaugural conference of the Greenleaf Centre for Servant-Leadership in Southern Africa. An intended 2-hour participative workshop was extended by another two hours the following day, due to the positive impact it seemed to have in building understanding of servant-leadership principles. The irony was that, apart from a brief Internet search, other speeches at the first day of the conference were really my own initial introduction to these principles! Yet, the resonance was clear, both with my own work up to then, and with the direction I saw leadership in the 21st century needing to take, in South Africa and internationally. I was fortunate after this to be asked to join the Board of the Greenleaf Centre Southern Africa, which encouraged me to continue my thinking about how servant-leadership principles could be of great use in the emerging and changing country. What was clear to me, however, was that the special situation of post-apartheid South Africa required a special approach that would be very different to how, for example, servant-leadership might be applied in the USA.

Since his release from prison on 2nd February 1990, Nelson Mandela has achieved a rare feat: his stature has, instead of being diminished by interaction in the 'real world', in fact grown. He is seen as the foremost statesman of his era, the Gandhi of the latter part of the 20th century. How is this possible? I would argue that it is precisely because of his pre-eminence as a great servant-leader. From the 'angry young man' of great charisma jailed 27 years before, he emerged from prison without bitterness, with a desire for reconciliation and forgiveness. Yet, his sense of justice meant he had refused being freed subject to conditions he saw as unacceptable ten years earlier. He was, rather, prepared to forget about his own life and stay in jail so as to keep the struggle alive. He furthermore put his leadership at risk by negotiating with the apartheid leadership at a stage when it was not accepted within the top structures of the then-banned ANC. He, unlike many other African leaders, stayed as president for only one term. He is always keen to claim that it was not his own input, but the input of thousands of others all over the country, that led to the demise of the old regime. In other words, he has little ego (but great personal authority), doing what needs to be done to build the country and its people.

Realising this, I found myself considering what it was that

135

allowed South Africa, where many had predicted a vicious bloodbath, to become a "light unto the nations", showing how peace and reconciliation are possible in the most difficult circumstances. Many leaders and Nobel laureates besides Madiba (Mandela's clan name) had provided outstanding leadership in difficult times. From Archbishop Desmond Tutu, to Chief Albert Luthuli, to Sir Laurens van der Post, a big influence on the thinking of Prince Charles, to Prime Minister Jan Smuts, who wrote a book called *Holism and Evolution* in 1917 that was 50 years ahead of its time, a precursor to the ecology and holism movement of the 60s and onwards. Smuts was a man of peace, but also a fêted war leader, part of the UK war cabinet in the Second World War and a close advisor to Churchill and the royal family.

The question thus occurred to me: what exists in South Africa to throw up such leaders that enabled the peaceful transition to the new democratic country, when in Sri Lanka, Israel/Palestine, until recently Northern Ireland, and other major conflict zones, the battles continue? The answer seemed to be that servant-leadership occurs naturally in South Africa; it is part of our history and way of being. It became clear to me, too, that I had been using servant-leadership principles unconsciously in some of the big change and transformation consulting projects I had been involved in up to then. In order to understand what I am saying, it is important to describe some basic concepts in our South African identity. I need to acknowledge the debt that I owe in this regard for the deep growth in my knowledge to my former mentor Mike Boon, a "white Zulu", under whose guidance I worked closely as a Senior Consultant for a year on his change and transformation project, Project Vuka (Zulu for "wake up!"), in a major bank with 8500 employees in 2001.

The first basic concept is **Ubuntu**, characterised by the saying in Zulu that "Umuntu umuntu ngabantu" – "A person is a person through other people." In other words, we are not only separate individuals, but part of an interdependent community that defines us and gives us breath. Hence, for example, the union slogan "an injury to one is an injury to all". In other words, we need to take care of all of us, black and white, together. For example, the African workgroup focuses first on moral and emotional elements, as opposed to the traditional western approach that is more on role and function. Building shared living values is central to the African approach. Forgiveness is a natural part of Ubuntu.

Many people mistakenly assume that being part of the collective means that all lose their sense of individual identity. But this is not so. There is, alongside, a concept called **Isithunzi** in Zulu. This literally means 'shadow', or dignity. The more you take care of your people, through doing good deeds in the interests of all, the bigger your Isithunzi. People want to be in your shadow. For example, Nelson Mandela casts a great shadow that many want to fall under, from ordinary people to kings and politicians, to rock stars. This seems to me the essence of servant-leadership.

Furthermore, while sometimes the western perception of African kings and chiefs is one of despotism, in fact in pre-colonial times the role of the chief was of gatherer of consensus, once all had participated and voiced their opinions. There is a Sotho saying that amounts to "A king is a king because of the people". In other words, these leaders reflected the needs and aspirations and voices of their people. If they did not do so, they might be removed. There were gatherings called Umhlangano's or Imbizos, where the people and the elders were consulted, either about specific issues or in general, which could go on through the nights until consensual decisions were reached.

One of the great leaders in this regard, King Moshoeshoe, lived through the turbulent period in the South African interior of the 1820s. Having fled from Shaka, the "Zulu Napoleon", his group had encountered starving tribes who had turned to cannibalism, such was their desperate plight after crops had had no time to be harvested and other fleeing tribes in turn displaced them. Some of his family had been captured in an attack and probably been eaten. Some time later, having established a powerful Sotho kingdom further inland on an impregnable mountain top called Thabo Bosigo, he would send out his scouts to invite other groupings to join him. One day, the selfsame cannibals were brought in to him. The expectation from his people was no doubt that they would be killed. But Moshoeshoe told them: "Inside the bellies of these people are our ancestors, they are the living tombs of those of us who have died. So, treat them with great respect." Moshoeshoe lived to be a great national reconciler and healer.

However, regardless of the great leaders that South Africa has thrown up, there are certain realities that still persist in this country, which have to be taken into account in any attempt to build a servant-leadership culture. From my work within corporates and government, it is very clear to me that two paradigms, two views of reality, exist in South Africa. At present they are seemingly irreconcilable, and require special attention in any change process. The first view is that of many whites, and of many in management. It goes something like this: "We are now in the New South Africa. We have to pull together on the same team. Workers must realise that, with the new global economy and the arrival of China as the workshop of the world, we have no choice but to be internationally competitive. If we are not, hundreds of thousands of jobs will be lost. This means we cannot afford high labour costs and serious affirmative action policies. There is no time to be lost. Let us move into the future together."

The opposite viewpoint, mostly of black South Africans and workers, goes something like this: "We waged a long struggle for democracy and justice in this country, and we won. Now we need to see the fruits of that struggle. That includes participating in decision-making within companies, and also increased wages that we can now live well on. This is our heritage. We are no longer prepared to be dictated to by management. We want ourselves as individuals and cultural beings to be taken seriously. The past needs to be redressed as a matter of urgency."

These two paradigms do not come just from a divided past, but reflect two totally different cultural views of the world. The traditional African view of time, for example, sees it as circular. To illustrate: the ancestors, those who have passed, live right here in the ground. If there is an ongoing issue that cannot be resolved in any other way, I may need to appease the ancestors by slaughtering a cow or goat, and they will then return to the point where the problem arose, and fix it. If this is done, I have a future. If not, I am a prisoner of the past. In contrast, the western/white perception of time is more linear, postulating a past that often needs to be left behind, "water under the bridge", in order to move forward. This was clearly illustrated internationally by the impasse at the World Conference on racism in Durban in the early 2000s. Addressing the issue of slavery, Western countries were generally unwilling to accept culpability, rather showing commitment to protocols ensuring that this would never happen again. The Third World, however, generally took the approach that there needed to be not only an apology, but redress for the past. There was little room for negotiation, and consensus was not found. The one paradigm focuses on forgetting, the other on remembering, as means to build a future.

Another field that shows the different cultural approaches – and there are many I could mention – is in the arena of values, often of import in servant-leadership facilitation. Let us take, as an example, the value of respect. In workshops, I will often ask if we understand what this means, and there is usually consensus that all in the multi-cultural group do. What becomes clear when I go further is that there is a danger of assumption. Often the dominant paradigm that has been established is that of management, of the previously white South Africa. However, in fact often what is perceived in different cultures as denoting respect requires the totally opposite behaviour. For example (and of course culture is not static and things are changing), when I ask them to act out who would walk through the door first in different cultures, for whites it is mostly "ladies first", for blacks the men enter first, mostly to ensure protection from potential danger. In many groups, white women have, for example, expressed irritation at black men who walk through doors and into lifts before them, seeing them as rude. And yet, amongst black people this is perceived as actually being *respectful*. There are many other subsets within this, such as whites needing much more personal space, whereas for blacks this is not such a big deal. Thus, a white person may feel imposed upon in a bank queue by somebody standing "too close". Other areas reflecting different personal spaces may be the need for whites to speak softly in buses and at work, respecting personal space, whereas for many blacks this is seen as gossiping – rather speak loudly so you may not be holding anything back. Again, it is a question of whites generally being more individualistic, blacks seeing themselves as part of the collective. For whites, it is personal space, for blacks, public space.

What I am trying to illustrate is the potential gulf that exists between different races and cultures. Moreover, this is often unconscious. Only when we focus on cultural differences, do the different worldviews become clear.

But it goes even further than this. Apartheid was a system predicated on building an innate sense of superiority amongst whites, and the opposite amongst blacks. In addition, it was a system that on a daily basis humiliated and hurt people of colour. From the Pass Laws, where most black people in urban areas were arrested at some time for not carrying a pass, to the authoritarianism of the 1970s and 80s, where the police and army were used as repressive instruments, many black people suffered grievously, with family members shot, beaten, or detained. It must be noted that whites did not escape some hurt, with many young males forced into an army that adventured in South and other parts of Africa, ending up suffering post-traumatic stress. Some white families were even part of the struggle. For example, in my own, two brothers left the country rather than do military service, one within the country was banned, jailed and beaten for his anti-Apartheid activities. I myself had to choose between doing two years of service for an army and a government that I did not believe in (and maybe being used as a troop to quell internal rebellion), going to jail for six years if I refused, or leaving the country surreptitiously for good. Not an easy or pleasant choice.

In other words, not only are there often unknown cultural differences, but also there is a huge backlog of 'baggage' – of pain, anger, fear – that is being carried in the present that needs to be dealt with. Only through discussion, dialogue and understanding can there be any rapprochement between the two paradigms of which I spoke. Any attempt to build a common approach, a unified team, a single corporate culture, will fail unless these gaps are dealt with first.

One of the ways this was done in South Africa was through the

Truth and Reconciliation Commission, the TRC, where victims and perpetrators of apartheid atrocities told their stories. To understand the importance of this, I would like to refer to the work of M. Scott Peck in his book *The Different Drum*[23] where he writes about building community. For Peck, there are four phases of this:

- Pseudo-Community
- Chaos
- Emptying
- Real community

Many companies and organisations are either in Phase 1 or 2. In Pseudo-Community, we smile at each other, seem to get on superficially, but underneath we have unresolved issues. Thabo thinks David is a racist. Sheila thinks John will not promote her because she is a woman. David cannot stand being told he is a racist, and having his authority questioned. When things get too hot, or we are under too much work pressure, we move into Chaos. Everything bubbles to the surface. When problems arise, an external consultant is brought in to run a team-building programme, and for a while things seem to be all right again. We are back into Pseudo-community.

However, in order to move into real community, we have to go beyond chaos into Emptying. In this phase we get to know each other as human beings. We get to understand our fears, our hopes, our differences and commonalities. There is a very moving story I heard in one of the first workshops I ran for the integration of the opposing armies. Let us call the speaker Petrus. He was the person who let others in a military medical base in at the gate. Before the diversity course he did with me as part of the Psychological Integration Programme (PIP) that many soldiers from different backgrounds went through, he was mostly ignored by those he let through. Then he told his story.

50 years ago, his father, who was a black albino, was being kicked to death by some farmers in the area. He, then a little boy of

---

[23] M. Scott Peck, *The Different Drum*, Arrow Books (new ed), 1990

10, ran to the police for help, but was told "Voertsek, kaffir!" ("Go away, Kaffir" – a highly derogatory word for blacks). He ran back, to find his father dying, and held him in his arms for his last breaths. His elder and only brother ran away, and he has never seen him since. This was the first time in 50 years he had told his story. Those who heard it could not fail to be unutterably moved. Having spoken it *and been heard*, his resentment towards whites, carried all this time, was healed. So, he was able to empty his bag, and move on. All those who did so, could move into a shared future. "Us and Them" became "We." A community was born. And there were many other stories to tell in many other workshops, from black and white, man and woman, management and worker. Once all the baggage, all the attitudes, perceptions, stereotypes about each other were laid bare, there was no more ammunition to hold back. From there, a real team could be built, based upon commonalities, and respect for differences and diversity. Previous foes became mutual participants in departments and armed forces, based on shared values and a strong desire for success of the organisation as well as the individuals it encompasses. The corporate culture widened to incorporate everybody's cultures. A sense of belonging was born. Productivity went up.

This story has been played out many times, in companies and government departments where I have worked. Much work has to be done, but what has been shown is that it *is* possible to bridge the gap between two seemingly totally disparate paradigms. What it takes is talking and dialogue, experiential workshops and follow-ups in the workplace that ensure participation by all, process-developed explicit shared values, a system of rewards for improved group and team productivity, and the willingness to open the corporate culture to all. And, of course, the courage from servant-leaders to recognise the divisions based on differences that may exist, even subtly, and the desire to do something about it, to move from adversarial relations to a real rainbow community we talk about but rarely live.

So, having said all this, it would be of use to describe a case study that encapsulates all of the above. This will show not only how we dealt with the divides of opposite paradigms as mentioned – essential in any servant-leadership programme – but also how we built the commonalities, the sense of common humanity, while at the same time achieving great results.

Delmas Coal is a small colliery based near Witbank, about 100 km east of Johannesburg. Within two hours of Johannesburg, the biggest and most powerful city in Africa, lies a large portion of the world's deposits of gold, platinum, coal and other precious metals. Over half a million workers are employed in mining in South Africa. For some time now, the colliery had been racked by negative relationships between workers, especially represented by the National Union of Mineworkers (NUM), and management. The initial workshop that was undertaken was, then, a relationship-building exercise between management and the three unions represented at the mine, held at a sleepover venue about an hour away.

Almost before I could introduce myself, the NUM regional organiser stood up, and noted angrily that he had not been told by management what they were doing there, and vehemently refused to be there "to play games while our hearts are bleeding". He announced that his delegation was therefore about to walk out. It took all my facilitation skills to convince him to stay, that my interests were of the whole company and not management. The process would allow an expression of what it was that was making hearts bleed, and a movement towards dealing with this by all. The discussion later on about servant-leadership also helped with the realisation that this would not be 'business as usual', that a fundamentally different approach was being advocated, in which leaders focus on the needs of their people first, helping to grow and develop them not just as employees, but as people.

By the end of two days, the very same regional organiser pointed at Pieter, the mine general manager, and told him: "I now trust you to take this whole change programme forwards". Merci, the HR manager, commented, "The relationship you have built between management and unions, after all these years, is nothing short of a miracle". The decision was taken, as part of this new partnership, to take the whole mine through similar workshops, approximately 20 at a time. This then commenced several months later and continued for most of the year.

The programme consisted of several aspects, mostly very experiential, mostly fun – although some parts required dealing with the past, sometimes a painful process along the way. The initial few hours focused on getting-to-know-you type exercises and trust-building. For example, the blanket fall, where one participant at a time falls off a raised platform backwards into a blanket held by others. The discussion that follows looks at issues of trust and control. For example, a leader needs to give up control and take the leap of trust that subordinates will catch her. Falling without trust, onto a small area like a rear end, makes it more difficult to hold, whereas a fall with trust, with a straight back, makes a person easier to catch. In other words, the learning goes, "trust starts with me".

Once sufficient trust has been built, the opportunity exists to start to deal with the baggage, through lists and discussions of what it is that negatively impacts on morale and motivation. Later, after working on lists of values that would be important in the workplace, and the power of vision (again, through powerful exercises, not just teachings), more time is spent on differences, on telling the often emotional stories of what people have gone through and are living in the workplace and at home, in the past and now. Emotional intelligence work helps them to understand the patterns of negative relationships that exist between themselves and others, and to communicate in ways that help build win-win solutions. Other money and pen exercises reinforce the lesson that we are all in this together; that either we all recognise this, or the whole company falls.

Once the differences have been revealed, the commonality of our humanity is explored, and then the celebration starts. Through singing and dancing, groups presenting role-plays and songs representing their cultures. Whereas before diversity may have been seen as a problem, now it is perceived as a source of great wealth. A company song is developed, and presented by groups. Finally, commitments are made to each other and the company, to all actively participate in the building of a new corporate culture in which all can feel they belong.

Coming out of each workshop – and it must be stated that invariably the teams would end up highly motivated, unified and passionate about the mine – would be a goldfield of information about what effects morale and motivation negatively.

Once all had gone through this two-day "Building Workplace Community" programme, this information was compiled, codified into areas of concern and fed back to management. This was where, especially, servant-leadership principles were discussed and enacted experientially. Following on this awareness, the information feedback was seriously tackled, and the willingness of management to address issues was a source of great pride to me. Whether it was the acknowledgement that most of the problems related to poor and often disrespectful communication with workers from management and supervisors, or that certain sections did not receive their weekly issues of soap, they were prepared to do something about as many as possible. The rest of the day was spent on action planning their intentions. Another thing that was done was agreement on the values that had emerged from the workforce. So, instead of the usual of management passing values down, that often are ignored, it was a bottom-up process that workers could see as 'our values'.

From the feedback, it was clear that both supervisors and management needed more 'emotional intelligence' work: How to get the best out of my people, in a way that they feel very happy doing it. This was agreed to, and workshops followed. In the weeks thereafter, an afternoon was spent launching the values, and also selecting the company song, from about 20 team entries, mostly from shop floor groups. I gave feedback from the workshops, totally unexpurgated, and sometimes gently critical of leadership. Again, I was given free rein.

The final step is the **Umhlangano** (Zulu for gathering or meeting) process, where natural work teams meet for two hours on a monthly basis to keep the values alive and work with any ongoing people issues that effect morale and motivation. This again is an area where managers need to give up control, as the process is facilitated by an external person initially, and then by a trained facilitator within the company, who probably will not be a manager. The group makes consensual decisions, where all have an equal vote. The great thing is that once control is given up, the process actually makes life easier for authorities, as the workers themselves are keeping alive the values, gently reminding transgressors that "this is the way we do things around here". The number of disciplinary processes usually sizably diminishes as a result.

In other words, managers and leaders, throughout the workshops, not only learn servant-leadership principles, but they experience how powerful a team can be when it is aligned, and all within it are taking responsibility for moving the team, and the company, forward. In other words, leaders can step aside and facilitate the growth and development of their people as workers and, most importantly, as human beings. Although we have facilitated 2-4 days workshops explicitly on servant-leadership in other companies, it was not necessary to do so here, as there was a long and ongoing process in which many of these principles were expressed.

The results from the Delmas Coal programme were apparent. We worked with the company for over a year altogether. From being 20% below target before we started, we were informed that production had moved to 20% above target once we had finished. The corporate culture was a much more relaxed, participative and happy one, where workers could be themselves; whole cultural beings who could express themselves fully. A very nice success story.

I have gone on a long rambling journey to show how the special circumstances in South Africa as a result both of a divisive past and also a paradigmatically opposite present, require a special approach. The much more individualistic approach of servant-leadership in the USA or UK, for instance, would not work in South Africa, where there is more of a collective reality, especially amongst black people and the poorer sections of society. In other words, developing servant-leaders requires both individual growth work and sensitivity to other cultures, to the past and present. What I am thus arguing for is a nuanced approach to the implementation of servant-leadership around the globe, as opposed to a "one size fits all" attitude. Just as the South African context has shaped my understanding and teaching of servant-leadership according to its own needs, different countries and circumstances require their own implementations.

In summary, the role of a servant-leader in South Africa is to recognise, reveal and help to heal the divisions that exist. A simple attempt to build a strong organisation without dealing with the past, and the underlying baggage, only leads to a reinforced "Pseudo-community". In addition, processes such as Umhlangano need to ensure sustainability of any change programme. servant-leaders in South Africa need to empower their people where they have been previously disempowered under apartheid, so they are no longer victims but co-creators of a new reality, a company that cares, enthused with Ubuntu. This requires courage and commitment. As I have expressed, though, once egos are out of the way, South Africa – which has risen to the occasion before – has the capacity to throw up leaders who can do this, shaped by the soil of Africa.

10

Servant-Leadership:
The Happy Story

Henry Stewart,

founder and Chief Executive of Happy

Happy is a training company based in the centre of London. Though still small, employing just over 50 people, we have won wide recognition. In May 2007 the Financial Times listed Happy as the second best place to work in the UK. In 2006 Business in the Community named Happy as having the most positive impact on society of any small business in the UK. In giving the award Prince Charles described us as "inspirational". In 2003 the company was rated the best in the UK for customer service, in the Management Today/Unisys Service Excellence awards. The winner is not allowed to re-enter for another four years but Happy was again short-listed for the 2007 version, renamed the Customer Experience awards.

This is all based on an approach I like to describe as 'management as if people mattered'. A guiding principle at Happy is that "people work best when they feel good about themselves". If that is true, and nearly all the people I've asked agree with the statement, it puts a new focus on management. The main role becomes one of creating a framework where people do feel good about themselves, and feel valued and motivated. This concept, of the primary role of management being to support their people is, of course, at the heart of servant-leadership.

Happy's history

I set up the company in my back room in Hackney (an inner city area of London) in 1990. It was then called Happy Computers and provided IT training. At the time most of the IT training sector was based on putting technical people at the front of the class and getting them to 'point and show', spending the day telling their students which button to press. It was not generally something which people looked forward to.

I wanted IT training to be a fun experience, leaving people feeling great and eager to go away and put their new-found skills into practice. Where others showed projected screen displays, we got people to be 'hands on'. Where others told people what to do, we asked guided questions, encouraging people to discover the answers and build their confidence in using the software. The approach can be summed up in the ancient saying, generally attributed to Confucius:

Tell me and I will forget

Show me and I may remember

Involve me and I will understand

Everything we do, in the training room and outside, seeks to maximise involvement and minimise 'tell and show'. For all this to work, for people to have a truly great experience at Happy, it is crucial that our trainers – and indeed everybody our customers come into contact with – are highly motivated and feeling great about working at Happy. I know it's working when our students comment, as they regularly do, on the great atmosphere and say they'd love to work here.

When people work at their best

When I work with people on how to create a great place to work (which is what our Happy People division does) I ask them to list

149

three key elements of management. Try it yourself. Imagine you have somebody newly appointed as a manager and you are telling him or her the key things they have to do to be a great manager. Jot down the three most important.

Most people suggest things like communication; setting clear objectives; being consistent, firm and clear; integrity, setting a good example. I then ask them to think about when they have worked at their best. Again, try this yourself. Think of a time when you are really proud of what you achieved. What was it about the environment, and how you were managed, that helped you?

In response to this exercise, people talk about being trusted and given the freedom to do things their way. They talk about facing a big challenge and about the support they received. I have asked thousands of people, at the training sessions I give and the conferences I speak at, about when they worked at their best. They range from Chief Executives of large organisations to front-line staff in low skilled jobs. But the answer is always the same – they virtually never give examples of when they were closely managed and told what to do; nearly every example is one where they were able to do it their way. If you gave an example like that yourself, remember that what is true of you is almost certainly true of your people too.

These two exercises ask the same question from two different sides. What makes great management should be what enables you to work at your best. And it is true that good communication and clear objectives are needed but they are not sufficient to create a great workplace. What creates a great workplace is what very few managers focus on: getting out of the way and giving people freedom.

Learning from *Maverick*

A key turning point for me came in 1993 when I read the book *Maverick* by Ricardo Semler[24], still in my (entirely biased) opinion

---

[24] Ricardo Semler, *Maverick*, Random House (new ed), 2001

the best business book ever written. Brazilian businessman Semler describes how he took over his father's business and found a company where trust was so low that workers were searched every night at the gates to check they hadn't stolen anything. By the time he wrote the book, workers were trusted to set targets, organise the workplace and in many cases even set their own salaries.

Maverick was a revelation. At the time Happy Computers employed just three people, but I was a typical stressed-out small businessman, working all the hours there were and phoning back every day from holiday to check everything was okay. *Maverick* taught me that there was another way, that if you got out of the way and trusted your people then they would grow and develop and you would get better results.

The change paid off. A year later I was off sick for three weeks and didn't phone in once. I returned to find just two phone calls I had to make. Everything else had been dealt with and sales had gone up. Since then every new member of staff has received *Maverick* to read and I've given away over 450 copies in total.

Let me tell you the story of how Happy Computers adopted this approach. In the very early days I was the only trainer. Modesty was perhaps not my strength and I was convinced I was the best trainer around. I saw that the challenge, as Happy grew, was to ensure all the other trainers were as good as me.

When I started to employ other freelance trainers I would sit in on them and make detailed notes through the day of what they were doing right and what they were doing wrong. And then I would sit down with the trainer and feed it back to them in great detail.

I was well intentioned, but you will probably have guessed that this did not go down well. More like a lead balloon, in fact. I was making two mistakes all too common in management. Firstly, I was trying to create a clone of myself, doing a job exactly the way I did. And, apart from its effect on motivation, this puts a ceiling on what can be achieved. The best a clone can be is as good as you. Secondly, I was trying to create a process, where people do the same each time. There is no room then for innovation or improvement.

At the same time I didn't want the trainers to do whatever they felt like. People came to Happy Computers for a particular style of training, fun and involvement. I didn't want them ever to sit and listen to a lecture, as was common at other training companies.

The job ownership model

Having read *Maverick*, I realised I needed to step back and put in place clear guidelines. So I sat down with the other trainers and agreed a set of principles such as "Don't tell when you can ask", still at the core of what we do. And we agreed a set of targets, based around the end of course evaluations. These were basically that the student had enjoyed the day and left confident in using the software.

The idea is that the principles and targets provide a flexible framework, which allows innovation. As a manager I am happy if my people are working within the principles and achieving the targets. I don't need to approve – or even see – everything they do.

We call our model 'job ownership' and there are a couple of extra key elements, as well as principles and targets. The first is support. There has to be somebody you can turn to if you are unclear, or are not achieving your targets. Most people need good attention from somebody who knows them well, to help them think and focus and also to set challenges. That person could be your manager. But the key is that the member of staff decides when they need them, not the other way round.

At Happy the management system was set up by Cathy Busani, who created and put in place all the support structures we have today. I left her to develop it and, at first, was confused to find that people were meeting their co-ordinators (our closest equivalent to managers) every fortnight. If we are about getting managers out of the way, I wondered, why were people seeing their managers so often?

Like many people, I had no good experience of supportive management, and have learnt how to work on my own initiative. My initial model had no clear basis of support for our staff. Many people felt isolated, and without the guidance they needed to succeed.

It is about management getting out of the way of day-to-day

detail, but very much being there to support and motivate our people. It addresses the common criticism of approaches based on giving people more freedom: that they also need more guidance.

I came to realise that the fortnightly meetings were effectively coaching sessions that people actually looked forward to. And that is crucial. If the meeting with your manager is not something you feel positive about, then it isn't providing the support you need.

The importance of feedback

Where do your people get feedback from about their performance? Many employees only get to hear how they are doing at their appraisal (every six months or every year) and then only from their managers, not from their customers (internal or external).

Let me draw a sporting analogy. How most people receive feedback is like playing a game of football and only finding out if you scored six months later. Even then you would only find out if your manager thought you scored. Think about that for a moment. How would even the great footballers be if that was the feedback they received? But that is exactly how we expect most of our people to work, only rarely receiving feedback on how they are doing.

At Happy we have a lot of feedback. We get feedback from the students at the end of the course and in a follow-up survey three months later. We have feedback in our online learning, and from those who call the telephone help-line. We have peer appraisal and upward appraisal. We have internal feedback on technical support and the operations team. This might seem like overload but it is all used to improve our service. And it is those who don't get enough feedback who complain, not those who get lots.

One of my favourite quotes is from ex-SAS Airlines Chief Executive Jan Carlssen: "Without information you cannot take responsibility. With information you cannot avoid responsibility." If you want your people taking real responsibility, you had better make sure the feedback they get is good.

Openness and transparency of information extends to every part of Happy, with the sole exception of any personal issues. This includes salaries. Every member of staff has access to a spreadsheet, which details not only current salaries but also every salary that every person has earned in their time at Happy. The approach is popular. In our last anonymous salary survey, we found that over half the staff had checked these figures in the last month and 86% said they liked open salaries.

Personally, I don't understand why companies like to keep salaries secret, unless it is because they know they are unfair. Having them open challenges managers to make sure every rise we give will stand up to public scrutiny. But it also fits in with Carlssen's principles. I want people to be clear what earns more income, and be focused on what the company does need. If your salaries aren't open, why not?

The benefits of job ownership

The result, 15 years on, is that the standard of training is far beyond anything I could have achieved. I am now rarely in the top half, on the company's quality ratings, when I do train. Two Happy trainers have been rated the UK IT Trainer of the Year, and three others have won either Silver or Bronze in these annual awards. No other company comes close to this record. I don't think I could have won those awards.

Those achievements have been the result of a good set of principles and, more importantly, the freedom to innovate within them. The result is that the standard of training at Happy nowadays is far beyond what I could have told people how to do. The trick is to make that framework crystal clear while giving people the freedom to work out their own way to achieve it – so it creates the landscape in which innovation prospers. And giving them the support and feedback needed to give them real ownership.

It was management guru Peter Drucker who said, "So much of what we call management consists of making it difficult for people to work." In contrast, when we won the award for the best customer service in the UK, we asked the judges what made them choose Happy. Their response was interesting. "You understand what your customers want. But that isn't unusual. Most companies understand what their customers want. But they then put in place a set of rules and procedures that prevent their front-line staff from delivering that. You don't. You give your people the freedom to do what is needed to give the customer what they want."

Don't approve it

We want to make it as easy as possible for people to do their jobs. So we try, for instance, to avoid having to approve things. Give people responsibility and let them take the decisions. A concept we particularly like is "pre-approval". If you set a group of people to come up with a new idea or to solve a problem, tell them it is "pre-approved". They will implement whatever they come up with, and nobody will seek to improve it.

Of course they need very clear parameters. You need to make clear the budget, you need to let them know who they need to talk to, any knowledge you have and any other parameters. We have used this in many areas. Three months ago I was at a trainers' meeting where there were complaints about the peer appraisal being cumbersome and not very effective. So I asked who wanted to come up with a new system, pre-approved.

A strongly motivated group has worked on it and the new approach goes live this week. I still haven't seen what they've come up with, but I don't need to. The right people were involved in devising it and, if it doesn't work perfectly, they will change it.

This approach applies to all staff. This year I have conducted exit interviews with two of our most junior staff, one who worked on reception and the other in our internal café. Both talked about how much they appreciated being given real responsibility and being able to decide how those areas looked and how they worked.

I recently received an email from one of our freelance trainers, thanking me for three recent changes that had made her work at Happy much easier. The first thing that struck me was that I was unaware that these changes had happened.

The second thing that struck me was that, if these changes had been put on my desk for approval, I would probably have rejected them. After all I set up this company, I was the first trainer and I originally set up many of the ways we do things. My natural bias is towards the methods I came up with.

Creating an excellent company is about lots of changes like this that steadily make life easier and better. The best way to enable this process of continuous improvement is to ensure front-line staff can implement changes without having to get approval.

As a result few things do come across my desk for approval. Occasionally, I am the only one with the skills and experience to decide on something. But that is rare. Generally I try and give the responsibility back. I ask, "What would you propose?" I try to avoid suggesting improvements and simply give the go-ahead.

Celebrating mistakes

Given responsibility, people will sometimes get it wrong. Just as I, or other senior managers, will sometimes get it wrong. To enable people to work at their best, a 'no blame' culture is crucial. We go further and seek to 'celebrate mistakes'. So if somebody comes to me, normally with a gloomy face, and tells me they've made a terrible mistake I aim to respond with "Great. Tell me all about it".

When Microsoft set up their research facility at Cambridge, the Director was told, "If everything you do succeeds, then you will have failed." Because clearly they would not have been taking enough risks or covering new ground if everything worked. I believe the same is true of front-line staff delivering day-to-day service. I want them to be trying new things and that means, sometimes, getting it wrong.

If a new member of staff comes to you at the end of their three-month probationary period and says "I'm doing a great job. I haven't made any mistakes", how do you feel? Either they are not being honest, or your support system hasn't made them feel safe enough to own up. Or worse, they have been playing it so safe that they genuinely haven't got anything wrong.

If somebody comes to me having messed up that day with one of our biggest clients I can sort it. But if I only find out two weeks later, especially from the client, it may be too late. And our people tell me that this 'no blame' approach genuinely makes it feel safe to take risks and try new things.

Choosing managers

I often say that our most radical belief at Happy is that people should be chosen to manage people ... on the basis of how good they are at managing people. It should be a truism but the reality is that people are normally chosen to manage according to how good they are at their core job or how long they have been around.

So if you have a programmer who is doing a really good job and has been in post for many years they are likely to be promoted to manager. Because the fact that they are really good at coding is sure to mean they are good at supporting and nurturing people. It wouldn't happen at Microsoft (which does very well in the Best Workplace awards), where a great programmer will be rewarded and incentivised to stay, but will not be made a manager unless they show the potential to be good at managing people.

And it wouldn't happen at Happy, where we believe that there are two manager skill-sets and it is a mistake to assume the same person should do both. On the one hand, skill set A – managers have to be good at strategy and decision-making. On the other, skill set B – they have to be good at supporting, coaching and challenging people. Often managers are promoted for skill set A on the basis that they will be trained to do skill set B (which is, it is widely assumed, really easy to learn...).

Ask managers whether they enjoy managing people and you will get two different responses. Half will say they love it, and it's what motivates them – the other half will say no, they don't feel good at it, it stresses them, and they'd rather focus on what they are good at. And this second half are the managers who people don't like working for, and leave companies to get away from.

In my opinion one of the most important things an organisation can do is find a way to promote and reward people who are very talented at their core jobs, without them having to manage people. In other words, playing to their strengths.

This is what we do at Happy. We have split the two skill sets, so some people are "co-ordinators", whose role is to support and coach their people. Others have strategic management responsibilities. There is overlap, with some people doing both, but this looser structure enables much greater flexibility.

Imagine somebody comes to you and says, "I love my work, I love the people I work with and I'm happy with my pay, but I can't stand my manager." What do you do? In traditional management structures it is difficult to deal with and the person will often end up leaving.

If it happened at Happy, it would take five minutes to sort out. We could simply find them a different co-ordinator. As co-ordinators are not tied into a rigid line management structure, it is easy to change them. The result is that people can get the support they need to do a great job.

The clubbing test

The point of servant-leadership is that organisations are most effective if the managers see their role as serving the people who work there. One of my favourite examples of this relates to flexible working. Happy was rated by the Financial Times in 2004 as the best company in the UK for work-life balance but in truth what we do is simple common sense. We seek to help all our people work the hours that make sense to them. In my talks I ask my audience which of these requests for a compressed 4-day week they would see as valid:

- They want to not work Mondays, to be at home with their baby
- They want to not work Mondays to study for a part-time degree
- They want to not work Mondays because they are exhausted after clubbing all weekend.

Most people agree to the first and generally also the second. But few agree to the third. The point I make is that it's not about them; it's about this individual. They should step out of making judgements on behalf of others.

We had this situation, where one of the best gay clubs was on a Sunday night and this member of staff was either tired or often absent. Their relationship with their co-ordinator was poor and they were losing motivation. So we agreed to them working their hours in four extended days from Tuesday to Thursday. The result was their absenteeism disappeared, their motivation soared and their workload increased. The company gained because we had put them first.

People often ask how we can judge competing requests for flexible working. The answer is that we try not to. With our smoothie department (smoothies = smooth operators = our admin staff) we laid out the parameters and left them to decide. We needed two people staffing the phones from 9am to 5.30pm. Within that requirement, they could choose their hours.

Everybody had negotiated what he or she wanted. Some worked compressed hours; some started early, some started late. Not only were the set hours covered but also, with some people starting early, the core hours were extended with the phones starting at 8.30am or even 8am. Once again, by putting our people first, we got improved service.

Still learning

We are still learning and still seeking to improve. But this people-based approach has brought clear benefits. In 17 years in business we have never lost a trainer, or indeed any member of staff to the competition. And recruitment is very cost-effective. We have over 2,000 people signed up on our website to hear about our next vacancy. Last time we needed trainers, I sent out one email and had 150 completed online applications within a week. We recruited five people with no external cost.

For the last two or three years we have been teaching other organisations how to work this way and have found the principles are easy to teach, provided that people want to learn. We recently brought together a group of managers we had worked with from a range of companies and they were very clear about the biggest benefit.

Managing this way is less stressful, and gives you more time to do what you are best at – whatever that is. By fully involving people, by keeping them informed and giving them freedom and responsibility (within clear guidelines) you end up not only with a more productive company but one less demanding of you. And all as a result of serving people! It's a paradox, but one that works. Try it yourself.

11

First Amongst Equals: An Interview with George SanFacon

Interviewed by Alison Feldman (Greenleaf Centre Australia) and John Noble (Greenleaf Centre UK)

Introduction

George SanFacon was Director of Housing Facilities at the University of Michigan, Ann Arbor, USA. When he took over, the 250-person department was managed in a traditional hierarchy. There were problems of low morale, low trust and burnout. George initiated a process of shared governance – the senior managers became the Facilities Council and traditional boss-subordinate relationships were eliminated. There was a shift from individual performance to emphasis on good faith and community. Four self-directed Management Teams were set up that reported to the Council. Decision-making was collective and done by consensus – an open book policy was adopted. The department's mission, goals and values are clearly stated and there are processes for dealing with conflict and lapses of trust.[25]

The mission statement is as follows:

---

[25] Facilities Council Handbook, University of Michigan

"Our Mission is to provide a building and service environment conducive to comfortable living and learning, while meeting our own basic needs for well-being and growth."

This is a simple and clear statement, which encompasses both the service to the customer, and also the needs of the workforce. Meeting those basic needs for well-being and growth at all levels led to the shared governance model.

This was an incredible unconventional step into an organisational world of co-operation and true servant-leadership. Robert Greenleaf argued long and hard against the concept of the single chief, with the corruption and loneliness this brings and loss of creativity.[26] The shared governance model at the Housing Facilities department is one that deserves to be widely shared as a blueprint for other organisations interested in addressing the pressures and shortcomings associated with a single chief.

George SanFacon truly aspired to live out the deeper meaning of servant-leadership. In this interview he shares some of his conclusions and thoughts about the needs of people for community and personal growth.

The interview

How did you come to question, at an early age, how the workplace was organised?

G. My first job was working part-time in a grocery store as a teenager. By the time I graduated from high school, I was working full-time on second shift in an auto factory. Since then, I've worked in a wide range of different jobs (security guard, short order cook, mechanic, teacher, facilities engineer, energy consultant, and operations manager) and different settings (factories, restaurants,

---

[26] Robert K. Greenleaf, 'The Institution As Servant', in *Servant Leadership*, Paulist Press, 1977

schools, libraries, colleges, and even on delivery trucks). From early on, and throughout my career, regardless of where I was working or what I was doing, I found the workplace experience and conventional organisational dynamic to be severely lacking, ranging from mediocre to a killing ground of the human spirit. Ironically, this significantly undermines what our organisations are ultimately trying to accomplish.

You use the term 'killing grounds of the human spirit'. Given your daily contact with young students, does this make you optimistic about the next generation of leaders?

G. Today's generation of young people have been dubbed "the millennials" by sociologists, and researchers claim that they are "the first great generation since World War II". Typically raised in small families, they have received a lot of love, attention and support. They have been very well cared for by their parents. According to the research, they have excellent values, and they work extremely well in groups, which I find very encouraging. I have a twenty-year-old son, Michael, who is a millennial, and I am very encouraged by what I see in him and his friends.

What were the events and people that you believe have had the most influence on you?

G. First, regarding *events* and, I would add, *circumstances*, my early experience with the conventional system and institutions played a major role in shaping me as a "counter-cultural." In terms of family, my father abandoned us when I was 12 years of age. My mother, who had been a housewife for twenty years, had to enter the workplace in middle age with three children to support. To make ends meet, she had to sell our house. At that time, divorce was relatively uncommon and not approved by the church. So as a single, divorced woman, my mom was isolated in the community. Raised in parochial schools, I had daily contact with a lot of people in the clergy who were not very spiritual – religious maybe, but definitely not spiritual. The predominant context and feeling for me in their system was *fear*, rather than *love*. As for education, I worked my way through college and graduated in Aerospace Engineering in 1970, the year that NASA's (National Aeronautics and Space Administration) budget was cut by 30%. So I ended up a new, unemployed engineer looking for work in competition with thousands of other unemployed engineers, most all of who had more experience than I did. After working my way through college and graduating in the top of my class from one of the most prestigious universities in the field, I took a job as a night-shift security guard, earning little more than minimum wage. Then there was the Vietnam War, which I could not bring myself to support, and I actively worked against US involvement via protests and helping to publish an underground newsletter.

So early on, there were a lot of events and circumstances that influenced and led me to question our conventional social systems and institutions. And probably because of that, I have been a reactionary and seeker. Like many others of my generation, I experimented with drugs and did a fair amount of them. This, of course, certainly reinforced a different way of looking at things! I've also done a lot of reading, which included learning about the world's wisdom traditions. This, too, affirmed a different way of looking at things, as well as "the small voice within". Over the last decade, the writings and work of Ken Wilber have been very influential. And lastly, as a formal leader and management professional, the writings of Robert K. Greenleaf (*The Servant as Leader* and *The Institution as Servant*) and Peter Block (*Stewardship*[27]) have helped me immensely in trying to live out the wisdom traditions in the workplace.

Second, regarding *people*, I had a wonderful friend, Carl, who was a fellow seeker. He passed away a few years ago, but prior to that and over a 30-year period we delved into a wide range of wonderfully rich materials and experiences, including mind-altering music, psychotropic drugs, yoga, Buddhist meditation, Holotropic

---

[27] Peter Block, *Stewardship: Choosing Service Over Self-Interest*, Berrett-Koehler, 1993

Breathwork, and other approaches for expanding awareness and altering consciousness. And I am still practising Vipassanna Meditation and, occasionally, doing some breathwork. My children, Alex and Michael, have been a great influence on me; more than anything, they have helped to me learn how to "let go" and live more generously. And over the last decade, I have had the wonderful support of my spiritual teacher, Barb Brodsky, and the good fortune of knowing Bill Bottum, the retired CEO of Townsend and Bottum, Inc. Bill has been a mentor for me in walking the path of servant-leadership. He was a student and friend of Greenleaf's, and was the first executive, I believe, to implement Greenleaf's "first-among-equals" model.

It is often the case that the ethos of a company depends on the commitment to its values by the current CEO, and can come to an end when he or she leaves. Is there anything that you have discerned in servant-led organisations that perhaps protect them to some extent from that?

G. Greenleaf postulated a great test for outcomes, which was: "Do those served grow as persons? Do they, while being served, become healthier, wiser, freer, more autonomous, more likely themselves to become servants?" So theoretically, with servant-leadership and the "first among equals" model, there should be an embedded capacity for continuity in caring, service and leadership. We will soon test that proposition in our organisation, since I'll be retiring next April. Actually, it's a completion of the work, because the participatory governance model we've developed over the years has not yet had to handle the challenge of continuity. My leaving will test the framework and provide an opportunity to further develop the model.

What advice would you offer your successor?

G. The advice I would offer my successor is: "Give the framework a chance, and listen to the counsel and wisdom of those who are already here. They have been working effectively in this model for over a decade, and they have been full participants in both governing and managing the enterprise throughout that time. As a result, there is a lot of embedded knowledge, expertise and capacity readily available."

In this regard, the work of Robert Kelly (*The Power of Followership*[28]) is worth noting. He claims that servant-leadership produces "great followership". And he defines great followership in terms of two dimensions – independent, critical thinking and active engagement. So a mature, servant-led organisation is comprised of independent, critical thinkers who are actively engaged on behalf of the enterprise. This, of course, would be a wonderful legacy and valuable resource for any organisation.

The "first among equals" approach, by its very nature, could be thought of as perhaps more open to the sort of conflicts that arise when personal antipathy or hurt feelings become portrayed as matters of conscience. What's the greatest lesson you have learned from dealing with these situations?

G. The greatest lesson for me is that handling differences and conflicts gets easier over time – that differences can come to be considered an *asset* rather than a *problem*. In large part, I believe, that's because of two factors in our system: (1) people have meaningful opportunities to influence and shape what is happening, and (2) they trust that they can be authentic without fear of retribution. Regarding the former, we work on the basis of consensus. (We define consensus, as "each member being willing to *fully* support a particular approach or decision". It may not be a person's first choice, but it is something he or she can fully support and own.) Regarding the latter, we make a distinction between *performance* and *good faith*. In our system, as long as you are working in good faith you are entitled to be a member of the community. Even if you are not performing well, you undoubtedly have basic redeeming qualities and ways to contribute. So if you're

---

[28] Robert Kell, *The Power of Followership*, Currency, 1992

able to work within our values framework, then we'll work it out; we'll switch job duties if necessary, or we'll get you some training, or whatever. But we're all in this together. So if you have a weakness or shortcoming that's significantly affecting performance of the enterprise and we don't correct it or at least compensate for it, then we are *all* vulnerable and at risk.

With these factors as context, there is less fear. And people can eventually begin to experience and come to view differences as valuable, rather than problematic. As Ken Wilbur puts it: "The problem in the world isn't that some people are right and some people are wrong. The problem is that everyone is partially right, and we lack the wisdom to create a larger truth that transcends but embraces all of the individual ones." So what can happen in the participatory model, or what's happened for us, is that people gradually come to appreciate and value differences. If we are having a conversation, for example, and someone is absent that brings a different or unique view to the particular discussion, their colleagues will sometimes say, "You know, it's too bad that so-and-so isn't here." They know that the lack of other voices and differing views is a limiting factor and handicap in addressing the matter at hand. Another thing we've experienced on occasion is what Stephen Covey (*The Seven Habits of Highly Effective People*[29]) calls "the third alternative". For example, we might each have a different idea about handling a particular issue. And in the process of working through to a consensus we come up with an entirely different approach that none of us had thought of beforehand, but is better than any of the individual approaches we originally brought to the table. Such experiences have helped a great deal in coming to appreciate and value differences.

The way you work in the Housing Directorate is different from the rest of the University. When you are recruiting, do you make that point to interviewees?

---

[29] Stephen Covey, *The Seven Habits of Highly Successful People*, Simon & Schuster, 1989

G. Yes. We tell job candidates, "We work in teams here." And they invariably say, "Oh, well sure, of course. I've worked in teams, too." And then we say, "No, you don't understand. We really work in teams here!" So we have a handbook and other materials to help people better understand the participatory nature of the framework.

In some organisations there exists a problem when senior staff or Board members are prepared to be inside the sphere of influence, but outside the sphere of responsibility. Have you encountered this kind of problem and how have you handled it?

G. We don't have a Board. We have a Council that runs the department, with twelve members on it. All Council decisions are made by consensus, and each member has full blocking rights on all decisions. But I am still held personally accountable by University executive administration for all decisions and outcomes. In that way, I have what Peter Block calls "accountability without control".

So there are higher levels of administrative authority that supersede the Council, including Executive Officers of the University and, of course, the government (through legal statutes and regulations). Where the Council is superseded by such, we simply comply with the requirements or directives. And since we know what the general boundary conditions are (University policies and governmental regulations), it is rare for higher-level administrators to intervene. In fact, I can recall only a few instances in the last decade. But when that happens, we handle it in an open, transparent manner. So the system is relatively free of manipulation and negative politics.

What gives you most satisfaction at work?

G. I feel most satisfied when a group process results in a way of handling something that no individual had thought of previously, but that addresses all of the issues and concerns raised. Another high for me has to do with healing, where some long-term brokenness or baggage in the organisation is worked through and resolved. And another, when someone stops by and says something like, "You know, I love working here. It's not so important that I make more money now, because I really enjoy working here. I don't know what's going to happen in the future or how long this is going to last, but I certainly appreciate it." That's a buzz for me!

We hear the phrase "work/life balance" a lot these days. Have you found the right balance for yourself?

G. I think now I have, but I'm divorced! So there was a time when I did not have balance in my life. Actually, it wasn't until we moved from an authoritarian governance system to a participatory one that I really achieved work/life balance. But perhaps "balance" isn't the right framing here, so I'll restate this. The participatory nature of our framework allows me to be who I really am and want to be. That being the case, I now experience my personal and professional lives more seamlessly. So it's no longer an issue of balance because they are no longer separate.

So the old idea of asking people to leave their personal problems at the door isn't something that would be tolerated?

G. We support people in bringing all of who they are to work. So if someone is having a difficult time at home or in their personal life, other people often know it and extend them extra support and understanding. Of course, it can be a problem if someone has long-term, chronic difficulties and always needs the extra support of the community. But all of us go through tough times now and again in our lives, and it's a relief not to have to mask or hide them.

But presumably you have had to fire people occasionally?

G. Yes, but we don't fire people for poor performance. Rather, we fire them for violations of good faith. (We define good faith as "demonstrating a sincere commitment to the mutual well-being of all affected parties." Each person on the Council or a Management Team signs a good faith charter, pledging to use their organisational position and power for the common good.) Removing someone from the community means they have grossly violated University policies or procedures, or they have failed to comply with repeated directives from their team. The process can be lengthy, and requires a community consensus that the individual violated good faith and warrants removal.

We often hear the phrase "spirituality in the workplace". Is that a phrase you use?

G. Well, I tried it once – and all hell broke loose! We are a public institution. Furthermore, we have people in the organisation from different faiths, as well as some that aren't from any faith, including atheists and agnostics. So I learned that using the term 'spirituality' can inadvertently exclude some people, thereby undermining the sense of community. We had to stop and consider this, and ultimately decided not to use the term. In the alternative, we use the term 'human spirit'. In that vein, we talk about the manifestation of the human spirit as evidenced by higher levels of morale, energy and commitment. We can promote that spirit by providing people "an appropriate workplace experience", which is comprised of three general requirements:

- *Meeting basic needs.* First, people are making enough money to provide themselves and their families with decent housing, clothing, food, education and health care. Their basic needs are met for living a material existence worthy of human dignity.

- *Providing society needed goods and services.* Second, people are providing society with *needed* goods and/or services. They're not making consumer "junk", carcinogenic products, or weapons. Rather, they are providing something they know is good for society, and they are doing it in ways that are good for stakeholders and those affected, including other living systems and future generations. So the work is meaningful.

170

- *Promoting enjoyment, well-being and growth.* Third, people have opportunities for personal and professional development, and the nature of the experience itself is enjoyable and fun. They can be authentic without fear of retribution, and they can influence what is happening and unfolding.

If these conditions are met, then the human spirit and life energy is more positively manifest, benefiting both the individual and the organisation.

It was once said that, "Organisations exist for the painless extinction of the ideas that gave them birth." Are servant-led organisations as prone as every other to not having the courage of their convictions?

G. I don't know. I do think that organisations and institutions are often formed with the intention to serve society and the common good. Over time, however, they develop their own "egos", or sense of existence as separate entities. Somewhere along the way, people leading the organisation come to view themselves more as stewards of the enterprise than as servants of the common good. So they avoid situations and decisions that put the organisation or institution at risk, even if it means betraying the core values and founding principles of the enterprise. This dynamic seems to eventually undermine almost all of our organisations and institutions, whether it's business, church or state.

What for you represents the clearest indication of effective leadership in an organisation?

G. The ability of people in the organisation to come together and effectively deal with a major challenge or crisis. The capacity for them to be able to appropriately frame their reality – that is, determine and clearly state what's *really* going on – and then collectively work out how they are going to respond and participate in what's unfolding.

How do you grow servant-leadership in an organisation?

G. At the individual level, I suspect that we *evoke* servant-leadership as much as we *grow* it. That is, that people have a basic goodness that becomes available to others and the community under the right conditions. As Wayne Muller put it: "The human spirit is naturally generous; the instant we are filled, our first impulse is to be useful, to be kind, to give something away." I have often witnessed this in our organisation when people have an appropriate workplace experience and meaningful opportunities to participate in creating and shaping what is unfolding. At the organisational level, we grow servant-leadership through a participatory governance system in which members have opportunities to meaningfully affect the life of the community.

Do you experience any problems using the phrases 'servant-leadership' or 'servant-leader'?

G. First, I don't talk much about 'servant-leadership' at the University. And we are quiet internally about our participatory approach to governance and management, which is very different than the greater University system. Nevertheless, executive administration has genuinely accepted and supported us. In large measure, that acceptance and support is contingent on organisational outcomes, which have been excellent. So, thankfully, we're able to do our work the way we want to do it.

Second, and more generally, I *have* encountered concerns or resistance on occasion with the term 'servant-leadership'. When I inquire about that, people claim that the terminology seems Christian-based and, therefore, exclusionary, or they have concerns about the meaning of the word 'servant' and its seeming inference to being 'servile'.

It really does look as if servant-leadership is spreading. Is that so, or are we just talking to ourselves more than we used to?

G. I think that a lot of us kindred spirits are connecting with one another through the language and community engendered via the movement. Most of us, I believe, already shared similar yearnings and consciousness before coming together under the servant-leadership tent. So in that way, we are probably talking more to ourselves that we used to.

As for the *range* or *reach* of the servant-leadership movement, it is certainly increasing. Word is definitely getting out. But I am more concerned about the *depth* of the movement. And by depth I am referring to the 'how' of servant-leadership, which, I think, has two levels – ways of being (for the individual), and the distribution of power (in organisations). In terms of the former, Greenleaf identified things like acceptance, healing, listening, community building, foresight, intuition and contemplation. In terms of the latter, he identified the issue of power in organisations, and promoted a *participatory* approach to governance (the "first among equals" model) rather than an *authoritative* one (the "lone chief" or boss/subordinate model). I think that the servant-leadership community needs to look more closely at how we can go deeper in living out servant-leadership and embedding it in forms of organisational governance.

When we talk about servant-leadership it is usually in the framework of the workplace, but I know that you always consider that in a much wider context. Can you say something about that?

G. Sure. Servant-leadership is not just about being in service to our employees, our customers and the institution. It's also about being in service to our local community, the environment, other living systems, other people around the world, including indigenous cultures, and even future generations. Servant-leadership is really about, I believe, what James O'Toole calls "the practice of moral symmetry", or what Ken Wilber refers to as "the expanded embrace".

Servant-leadership is clearly a values-based approach. Did you use any intentional processes to help you reach a common understanding of what that values-based approach might look like?

G. First, I think that *all* approaches are values-based. Think of Hitler! I would claim that he had a values-based approach, although most of us abhor those particular values. So, it's not values *per se*, but *what* values or *which* values we are aspiring to and striving to live out.

In our case, we *did* use an intentional process to develop our mission statement, a shared commitment, our overarching goals, and a values/beliefs statement. Those values include: *service, change, connectedness, the person* and *balance.* Our work together on developing the values list included crafting definitions of each value to further our common understanding. Additionally, each member of the Council and Management Teams has signed a charter pledging themselves to uphold and live out these governing ideas and aspirations.

Do you think that the students in your community are drawn to the same values, or do they hold different values and, through your approach, do you make an impact on them?

G. I think there are universal values that are held by most everyone – values people would like to see manifest in their experience and in the way they are treated. If that's the case, then I would guess that we affirm and resonate with student values.

What about the staff?

G. When it comes to staff, it's not the values that we have written on the mission statement that matter; it's the values embedded in the nature of their experience with the system and its leadership. If those values are affirming and life-giving, then I believe that staff will also live them out and pass them on to those they are serving.

In passing on these values, what sorts of things do you see happening or what are some of the behaviours that might be an indication of them?

G. What I see is *caring* – that is, people doing things that indicate they are generally concerned about the well being of others.

And what would you say are your personal values?

G. Promoting human well-being and growth in balanced ways.

There is a resonance between the work that you do and your core values. Has it taken a while to find that place where it resonates?

G. It took me a very long time, and I had to take a major risk in changing our governance system to achieve it. As I mentioned earlier, throughout my career I found the workplace experience lacking. So when I got into management in the early 1980s, I began reading a lot of management literature in search of alternatives. But it didn't seem to address the deeper issues. I did find a lot of material on self-directed teams (SDTs) that resonated with me, but our managers were resistant to implementing them. Eventually, I decided to implement my own self-directed team (the Council) by collapsing our uppermost levels of management into a circle of peers to govern and manage the enterprise. All of this coincided with my mid-life passage (it helps to call it a passage, rather than crisis!), during which I was on the verge of a nervous breakdown. It was resolved by creating a governance framework that was consistent with my own core values, a framework based on *love* rather than *fear*.

Do you think that sometimes it's all a matter of people trying to find the organisation where they can work and resonate?

G. I think the basic problem is that our workplaces are typically authoritarian. And authoritarian systems are generally not a good fit for human beings or the human spirit. So there are not a lot of real alternatives for people. In most cases, the best you can do is find a *benevolent* authoritarian system, rather than an *exploitative* one.

One way that organisations have tried to change the system has been to include their values and vision in the mission statement. Is it your experience that that has made some impact?

G. I think including the values and vision in the mission statement can have either a positive or a negative impact, depending on the level of integrity that the organisation achieves around them. Unfortunately, many of us have a lot of experience with organisations and institutions claiming one set of values (people-based), but actually living out another (material-based). This undermines trust, promotes withholding on the part of individuals, and leads to cynicism. In striving for integrity, I have found "compassing" to be very helpful; that is, using the values and vision statements on a day-to-day basis for the business at hand. That can be done by simply and openly asking the hard questions when deciding to do something. Does this action reflect our values? And does it move us toward our vision? This can be very challenging, but it can also help immensely in staying on track.

I remember a sports writer who had the line that if you really value something you can use the "so what" test. Someone says, "Your daughter has a vocation, and that vocation is to study at Purdue University in the United States. But it's going to cost you a fortune." Now, if your value is money, you say, "How much?" But, if your value is promoting your daughter to being who she is, you say, "So what?" And you move along. I think the mission and value statements are very important, but what is the process that holds integrity around that?

How can we shift the system to allow universal human values to come in?

G. I think that we need to deal with *power*. As Bertrand Russell put it: "The fundamental concept in social science is power. In the same sense that energy is the fundamental concept in physics." For organisational and institutional systems, that means addressing the conventional one-on-one boss/subordinate model (or "lone chief" model) that Greenleaf spoke against, and moving the governance system from an authoritarian one to a participatory one.

The work of Ken Wilber is worth noting here. He claims that increasing levels of hierarchy are about increasing levels of wholeness and integration, not dominance and control. So hierarchy, *per se*, isn't bad. What *is* bad are the pathological forms of hierarchy – specifically, *dictatorships* (the one dominating the many), and *totalitarianism* (the many dominating the one). As a form of dictatorship, the boss/subordinate model is a pathological form of hierarchy. In the past, slavery was common but is now unthinkable. In the future, authoritarian systems and the boss/subordinate model will be unthinkable, too. Just like clear-cutting a rainforest will be unthinkable.

Do you think there are major differences between cultures in this need to find work with connection to values?

G. I doubt it. While the particular values may differ across cultures, I would guess that the underlying need to align work with values can be found in all cultures. After all, work is not a separate field of existence in our experience, but an integral part of our daily lives.

In Western culture, I believe, most people want pretty much the same thing. As David Bowers put it: "We each want appreciation, recognition, influence, a feeling of accomplishment, and a feeling that people who are important to us believe in us and respect us." We want to have significance, to influence what's going on around us, to make a meaningful contribution, and to be recognised and appreciated for such. And we want to be who we are, not having to hide parts of ourselves or pretend to be somebody else. We want to live out loud!

Note: George SanFacon can be contacted at: gasanfan@umich.edu

12

Love and Work

A Conversation with James A. Autry

Some time ago, John Noble, Director of the Greenleaf Centre for Servant-Leadership United Kingdom, and Larry Spears, President and CEO of The Greenleaf Center for Servant-Leadership in Indianapolis, met with James A. Autry in Des Moines, Iowa. What follows is a record of the conversation that took place.

JOHN NOBLE: *Jim, you have had a profound effect on the attitudes and actions of huge numbers of people through your work. What were the markers in your life, the people and events that have helped shape your thinking?*

JAMES AUTRY: I feel that everything is connected, every experience and relationship is connected, and somehow they all point in the same direction. So I go back to people in my childhood who were people of good values who had a great influence on me in a very difficult situation – my parents were divorced, and I lived in a federal housing project in Memphis with my mother. These were some of the personal influences that shaped my values along the way.

And then I learned in the Air Force – which we all think of as a hierarchical structure – that the best leaders, the ones who seemed to achieve the best results, weren't the ramrod-straight, "kick 'em in the rear" sort, but the ones willing to get out among the people to identify with them. The best squadron commanders were the ones who regularly flew, who didn't just sit behind a desk, who mingled with the pilots and had a more personal relationship with them. I also found that they didn't have any more problems with discipline than the ramrod-straight ones did, and that had an influence on me.

Later, when I went into business, it was very clear to me that the people who were the most effective managers were those who were thought of as the weakest by higher management. This always troubled me, because if the objective was to achieve results, why was there such an emphasis on behaving a certain way? It was as if the results themselves were worthless if the managers didn't conform to what was perceived to be a management attitude. I think I learned from that. When I became a manager – at twenty-nine, I think I was the youngest managing editor in the history of *Better Homes and Gardens* – I thought the way to do it was to adopt the hierarchical attitude. It didn't work for me. I tried, but it wasn't me and it didn't work.

Then along came a man named Bob Burnett, the CEO of the Meredith Corporation. In 1968 he made a speech about self-renewal. This was a top corporate manager – one of the most courageous ones I ever saw – and he made a speech to the management group about self-renewal. As he went through the list of all the things about self-renewal, he said, "The most important thing is love." That was the first time I had ever heard the word 'love' used in the context of corporate life. This was 1968, and he spoke of love – love of what we do together, love of ourselves, love of our customers, love of our products. He said we could not renew ourselves without love. The company really was in need of renewal, and I saw his leadership turn the company around. He became a mentor to me, and that probably marked the beginning of the end of my transformation.

That's when I completely let go of the old ways. In the next several years I tried to integrate that love into the corporate setting. And it just kept working; I just kept getting results. We went from $160 million in revenues to $500 million; we went from four magazines to seventeen magazines during that period, and it was all about supporting people, being a resource to people and letting the vision evolve from the organisation, rather than enforcing the "top down" vision. These were my markers. They started with values. I'll tell you something else I've learned: there's something about being at the bottom of the economic totem pole, and it seems to me it goes one of several ways. With the grace of God, a good mother, and several other influences, I went in a good direction. I learned that if you can retain the feeling of what it feels like to be a "have not" in a society of "haves", to be down in the hierarchy, you can carry that with you into leadership positions. I think it makes you a more effective leader. So don't forget where you came from. In *Love and Profit* there's an essay called 'Management from the Roots'.[30]

LARRY SPEARS: *Can you tell us about three or four authors or books about leadership that you have found particularly useful?*

JAMES AUTRY: I'm not just saying this because you're here, but Robert Greenleaf's work has had a great influence on me. Before discovering that, I was influenced a good deal by Warren Bennis, not just by his writing but by the man himself, in his seminars and workshops. I'm taken by Peter Block and Peter Vaill, especially Vaill's book *Managing as a Performing Art*.[31] These are the people that just jump to mind. I have a library full of leadership books. And it's interesting, I get something out of a lot of them, and yet I find that the totality of the work often doesn't appeal to me, but something in there does. But Warren Bennis's work, Peter Vaill, and, although it's a lot to work through, Peter Senge's *Fifth Discipline*[32] and his whole learning organisation work I've found very helpful. I've used some of the exercises in Senge's books to help achieve some honesty in a community setting. I've never met him, but I've seen videos of him, and he seems to be what his work reveals. I guess that's what jumps to my head. Oh! Of course! Margaret

---

[30] *Love and Profit: The Art of Caring Leadership*, James A Autry (Avon Books reprint 2007)
[31] *Managing as a Performing Art: New Ideas for a World of Chaotic Change*, Peter Vaill (Jossey Bass 1991)
[32] *The Fifth Discipline: The Art and Practice of the Learning Organisation*, Peter Senge (Random House Business Books revised ed 2006)

Wheatley for *Leadership and the New Science*,[33] that whole notion of everything in relationships and everything affecting everything else, the model from quantum physics. And then there are people who've not written on leadership but whose work has had an influence on me, like Joan Borysenko and Scott Peck. I've enjoyed Joan's work, and Scott Peck's original *The Road Less Travelled*,[34] and subsequently meeting him and working with him has been a very positive influence on some of the things I've done on leadership.

LARRY SPEARS: *Leadership concepts, including servant-leadership, values-based management, learning organisations, and similar ideas are being learned, taught, and practised more than ever before. What do you see as the cultural changes that have caused these ideas to be more widely accepted?*

JAMES AUTRY: Well, we have to qualify the answer by saying that there are still some industries where none of this is being done, like in Detroit, the oil industry, and some of the heavier manufacturing industries. I don't think it's because they have union people; I think it's just that the culture hasn't shifted. Now, it may be that within departments or within groups you'll find these values. I work all the time in companies you wouldn't think of as being particularly servant-leader oriented or values oriented, and yet within a group it's very much alive. So I see it as a positive virus in these businesses. But there are companies that are wholly committed. I am not a sociologist, only an amateur social observer, and anything I say on the subject will be obvious, but clearly one of the cultural shifts has been the increasing number of women in the workforce. There are two factors that come into play. One is the impact of motherhood and women's need to balance this, and the other is scientifically based, the idea that women socialise by affiliation, whereas men socialise by separation. That makes a profound difference on how their work

---

[33] *Leadership and the New Science: Discovering Order in a Chaotic World*, Margaret J. Wheatley, (Berrett-Koehler 3rd edition 2006)
[34] *The Road Less Travelled: A Psychology of Love, Traditional Values and Spiritual Growth*, M. Scott Peck (Rider & Co. Classic Ed edition 2008)

styles will be manifested. These are generalisations, of course. You will find women who are hard-edged and tough, and men who are sensitive and supportive, so I don't want to overgeneralise, but I do think these differences have had a major impact in the development of workplace culture, especially in helping to create a medium in which concepts that are more affiliative and communal and more supportive of workers and less hierarchical can grow. I think the presence and influence of women is certainly a factor.

I think another factor is that so many people have seen that the old ways simply don't work as well as this stuff. There's been a feeling of frustration that "I can't get the results that I want to get" that leads to openness to writings and influences from the media about another way to do it, so that's been a factor. The challenge of how to get results has permeated management generally as compensation systems have shifted for CEOs and have created a downward pressure from CEOs to enhance stock price. *Stockholder value* has become the mantra, and in the end that is defined as stock price. So the emphasis on results has created fear and frustration on one hand, and a desire to try almost anything to get better results on the other hand. And that creates an approach to change that's phoney: "Well, I think I'll try the soft approach now and get them to work a lot harder." You have to be careful about that; it's got to really come from the inside of a person. But it does seem to me that society is more open to it.

Many company leaders are concerned about loyalty and turnover. This also creates an interest in values-based leadership. What's been proved over and over again is that people are not going to work where they feel driven or unhappy. They work hard (and I think people are working way too hard doing unnecessary things), they're putting in a lot of hours, but they're not doing it because managers are kicking them in the rear and making them do it. What does that mean if you're trying to hang on to people in a highly mobile culture? How do you create culture, how do you do things that bind them, that make them want to stay someplace? What works is creating community, even if people say "Yeah! But they're not going to be here very long." This is a lesson I learned in the Air Force.

People rotate in and out of squadrons and highly intensive settings all the time. Personnel are changing all the time; in fact, the most you get is a three-year tour. There's a very intense and intentional imperative toward creating a community, then people come into these communities, they're brought into it, and immediately become a part of it. They may be only there six months, but they're no less a member of this community and they feel no less committed to it. I have seen it work in that kind of setting, and I know that it can be done. And the businesses that are building community are the ones that are holding on to employees the longest, regardless of what the compensation structure might be.

JOHN NOBLE: *One situation I think we are familiar with is that in which the CEO of a company is very willing to make the change toward more values-based management. The junior managers are gung-ho for the whole idea, but it is in the ranks of middle management where the resistance, not surprisingly, exists. What advice or guidance do you offer companies in this situation?*

JAMES AUTRY. I think the situation starts with an analysis. Part of the analysis is this: the reason is fear. So what are the middle managers afraid of? They are afraid of the loss of power, perceived power, the loss of their jobs. If everything goes well, they might not be needed. In order to make this change, you have to address the fear issue in the middle manager. Let's face facts – in the great wave of white-collar layoffs, it was the middle managers who got the axe, so they've got good reason to be afraid in view of what's been happening in the last fifteen years or so. If the CEO is gung-ho on it, it's on the CEO to bring it about.

I think it has to be done by building a sense of community based on trust. The middle managers have to feel that they are a part of bringing this about, that it's not being foisted on them. It's a huge education process for them because a lot of them got where they are under the old ways. "The old ways worked for me; why change?" So there's a re-education and a reorientation process needed, and at the same time there has to be a reaffirmation that they got there because of their knowledge and competence, not because of their management style, not because of authoritarianism. What we're going to change is the culture, the social architecture, and the interpersonal relationships. We're not going to change the positions, the account-ability. We're not going to change the results we want. But the fear has to be taken out, and that's an education process.

I've been involved in this in three companies and, I'll tell you, it's a tough nut to crack. Managers have been brought up in an atmosphere of they don't trust people, they don't feel trusted, they don't trust the company. It's a long process and it's a difficult chal-lenge. I think it takes community building, it takes personal attention and commitment from the CEO, because on the one hand he's saying, "I'm going to need these results," and on the other hand he's saying, "We want to be this kind of company." He's got to somehow communicate that "I think that creating this kind of company is going to give us these even better results. Trust me on this, let's do it." This takes leadership from the top. You can't delegate this kind of cultural change.

JOHN NOBLE: *Thinking more about these young leaders, what are two skills or characteristics you would wish them to have?*

JAMES AUTRY: Let's call them characteristics; because I never try to tell people what to do, I try to tell them how to be. I think they have to be empathetic, that's one of the characteristics. Can I give you five? The five are be authentic, be vulnerable, present, accepting, and useful. And by *useful* I mean be servants. Those are the five characteristics. And underneath all that they have to be courageous, they have to show that vulnerability and authenticity, and empathise and listen – that's all part of it. One of the first things I say to groups when I speak to them is: "I'm not here to tell you what to do. You know what you should do much better than I could ever know."

JOHN NOBLE: *One of the things I often find myself talking to col-leagues about is the joy of what you once called leaving work and being able to say, "I did it well today." What were the circumstances that usually led you to be able to say that?*

JAMES AUTRY: It's always been relationships. It's always been if somehow at the end of the day I've managed to create a sense of community, and have either resolved conflicts or created circumstances in which they got resolved. It's always been about personal relationships. Now, am I really happy when we start a new magazine, or we got a good sales result, or we turned the corner and made a profit? Yes, I really am, and that gives me an enormous sense of satisfaction. But I have always seen those results – even my own salary – as simply the tangible measurement of the real work. That's not the real work, making profits. This is one of the great distortions in American business life. The real work is not making profits; making profits is the result of the real work. So I get enormous satisfaction from that, and great satisfaction from the doing that's done. But when I felt *I did it well today*, it's always been relationships, even if it was just convening a good meeting filled with ideas and energy. That could make me feel good because I realise that people felt confident enough to be able to say things, knowing that they might not work, without fear of ridicule or fear of being shouted down.

Lately, in the last several years, the greatest feeling of satisfaction I've gotten is when I've been called to go into a company to resolve conflict between people. I've done a lot of what's now called executive coaching and counselling, and a lot of this is listening to people talk about the things that trouble them most deeply in their personal relationships. But conflict resolution is getting people who are at odds with one another – vociferously and sometimes angrily at odds with one another – bringing them together and getting them to make a human connection. You realise that underneath the differences in ideas, they are more similar than dissimilar. They have joys, fears, griefs, and celebrations that are more similar than dissimilar. Because they have different views of how the work has to be done does not make them enemies.

And it's that old dualism, and we fight the dualism all the time – you know, "If you're not for me, you're against me." We know from Biblical scholarship that that's not exactly what Jesus meant, but it gets quoted all the time. "If you're not with me, you're against me." That dualism of defining myself by the other, by who I'm not, permeates business. People have disagreements over all kinds of things like budgets or sales presentations. Some things that require disagreements, perhaps to shape them to the most effective way of doing business, turn into personal warfare. Well, it gives me an enormous sense of satisfaction to help people accept one another as human beings, even uneasily at first, and know that they can disagree about ideas without demonising one another as fellow human beings. Sometimes I let these discussions become heated because it's necessary to get some of the feelings out on the table where they can be dealt with.

JOHN NOBLE: *I'd like to ask you about one of the old chestnuts – "I don't have to be liked to be an effective leader." What are your views on that?*

JAMES AUTRY. The way you hear it in America often is, "Look, management is not a popularity contest." When a manager would say that to me, I'd say, "Well, to a certain extent, it is." It's not that you have to be the jolly, well-liked, "hail fellow well met", but if people don't respect you – and that's the operative word – if they don't respect you and your abilities as a person, it's not going to work for you. What I think and what I've often said is, we don't really have to love one another to work together. In fact we really don't have to like one another. We don't have to walk out the building and commingle, have drinks or party or anything. But in this kind of place we have to care about one another. That's kind of an interesting concept, to say we don't have to love one another, just care about one another. Because you have to care about what we do together, because what we do together is interdependent. We need to care about one another in the context of what we do together. That's a difficult concept sometimes for people. If people like one another and care about one another – genuinely – outside, then so much the better. I've always promoted that sort of personal connection. I've always been against the idea that "I have to remain aloof from the people, and it doesn't matter if they like me or not, because I might have to fire one of them." So I may use a different vocabulary in saying this, but respect and caring in the context of what we do together is essential. Whether you have personal likes or not is neither here nor there.

186

LARRY SPEARS: *In* Confessions of an Accidental Businessman[35] *you wrote, "The commitment to act out beyond ego, to recognise when we are in denial, to retain humility, to correct our mistakes and to learn from others, regardless of their so-called status, is the commitment to grow personally and spiritually through the work we've chosen to do." To me that really captures the essence of servant-leadership, at least in my own understanding of what servant-leadership is about. Would you talk about how one goes about overcoming ego in a leadership position?*

JAMES AUTRY: That's a good question: How do you overcome ego? The first step toward overcoming acting out of ego, I think, is to recognise that you do it, and to be able to identify when you are doing it. I think the only way to get out of the ego is to get into yourself. You have to have some sort of spiritual discipline – meditation, prayer, yoga. I am always recommending to people that they do something to nurture the inner life, that they try to do something every day that is reflective or meditative, even if they do it while they're jogging or walking. In order to get out of the ego you have to somehow get deeper into your own inner life. And I think you do that through the spiritual disciplines of silence and prayer and meditation. Or by reflective and meditative action, and by that I mean you can jog meditatively. I do it. I walk that way. You could also do psychotherapy or counselling, or meet with groups or just meet sometimes like with these groups where high-level businesspeople meet to, discuss their mutual problems.

Once you recognise it and begin to work on it, you have to stop throughout the day and examine what your actions are. In order to be able to admit mistakes and to learn from others, no matter what their status, the piece of advice I give to everybody – in fact, it's the same advice I offer every manager, new or old – is this: Whenever you attempt to make a statement, ask a question. Instead of saying "Here's what you should do," you say, "What do you think we should do?" That's a huge leap for a lot of people. It seems simple to say it, doesn't

---

[35] *Confessions of an Accidental Businessman: It Takes a Lifetime to Find Wisdom*, James A. Autry (Berrett-Koehler 1996)

it? But it's difficult for us to fathom how challenging that is for some people who act out of ego. Because you are saying, "Put my ego in the drawer and I'm gonna ask how you think it should be done – you, who are seventeen layers down in the hierarchy from me."

The next step is to do that not just as a technique, but to recognise that you're open to learning, and that the other person may know the thing to do. My attitude about this is, if an employee comes in and says, "Jim, here's the situation and this is the problem and I'm laying it out and what do you think we ought to do?" then I know that person already knows what to do. They've got the situation surrounded, they have the problem defined, and they, whether it's a group, or just a he or she, they know what to do – probably. If not, they've got a good first step. And I may know what to do, too, because I've been in this long enough, I can see all the pieces, it fits together, and I know what has to happen. And I know they have a step. They know that I know. But as soon as I fulfil the expectation that I'm going to be "Big Daddy" – you know, I'm going to make a pronouncement and they're gonna go do it – I've destroyed any possibility, one, to learn something from them and, two, to recognise their own power, which is their knowledge and their skill and which is real empowerment. Empowerment is not about "I take some of my power and give it to you." That's the myth. Real empowerment is recognising that you, by your skill, your knowledge, your commitment, you already have power. What I'm trying to do is take the leashes that I've put on, off.

So by that simple technique of asking a question instead of making a pronouncement, we can start to come out of ego. Another step toward acting beyond ego is to let go of my solution and embrace someone else's. Any number of solutions may work. They may not work as well as I think mine would work, but if one will work and achieve the result, then let go of ego and embrace the other solution. All our management structure traditionally is built on the basis of the person up here who has all the answers. What I keep saying is, don't be the person who has all the answers; be the person who has the best questions. And then you'll get better answers!

LARRY SPEARS: *You mentioned doing work in the governor's office, and your wife is Lieutenant Governor of the State of Iowa. I was curious to know whether past experience, or even more recent experience, has led you to any sense regarding whether there are differences between leadership as practised in politics versus business or organisations. You've written a great deal about effective leadership in the business setting. Do you see any differences when it comes to that kind of leadership within the political structure?*

JAMES AUTRY: I think leadership in public service is more difficult. It is a good place to practise servant-leadership. American people seem to want a field general in their leadership positions, yet the most effective leaders have been the ones who really practised community and consensus building. It's really the only way to get anything done – I've learned that from the inside, just seeing this process. I realise that the most effective public servant-leaders are those who know how to get people together and build a consensus; who interpret and articulate what they are trying to accomplish; and who tell why and how they are doing it for the people, for the voters.

It's a much more challenging kind of leadership than in business, because in business the objectives are very clearly defined. One, the most imperative objective is survival – not survival at any cost, not sacrificing your values for survival, though some have done that – but survival. Second, you need to achieve the objectives of the business, which some people define as *stockholder value*. Once you define the objectives of the business, they are pretty concrete, they don't shift very much. There may be market changes and things like that, but you're still trying to achieve these objectives. The constituency you have may be millions of stockholders, but they're represented by a board of directors of twelve or fourteen people, and they're the ones you have to convince. So finding the leadership of the employee group is, I think, less challenging in business because you have such flexible tools. You have compensation systems; you have hours and benefits; you can try all sorts of modes of structuring the office, from the virtual office to flexitime. You find you have a vast array of tools that you can use, if you're courageous enough to use them and smart enough to use them.

In public service, all the employee rules have been set by legislation, and are managed by agencies and work under legislative oversight. It's a very complex management challenge. There are posts that the governor comes in and appoints, then these appointees hire more positions, and then agencies get permeated with people with one political philosophy. Legislation changes, political philosophy changes, and it's very difficult. We've heard that democracy's messy. Democracy's very messy! It's a good system, I like the checks and balances. I think that it generally serves the people, but it could serve them better if we could get better public perception and understanding of what the real objectives are, what we're really trying to accomplish, rather than all the peripheral things. And, in that, I blame my old business, the media. They are forever doing an injustice to the system by jumping on things that are of relatively little consequence when it comes to governance and the objectives of society. So, yes, I think political leadership is far more difficult. Yet there are some good people on both sides of the aisle. They're good leaders, they're good about the vision, they're good about consensus, they don't let their egos paint them into a corner, and they don't demonise others.

In politics there's a lot of demonising. Having grown up a fundamentalist Christian, I understand those folks and what they want. But, as I say to my relatives in Mississippi, the US Constitution is about equality and justice and opportunity. It's not about righteousness. There was no intention for us to become a righteous nation, but a nation governed by people whose values – perhaps even whose righteousness – was based on their faith – probably. Wouldn't *have* to be. You can be moral without religious faith, you can be an atheist, but for the most part, these values are based on faith. But the objective of the Constitution is not to be a righteous country; even George Washington said that America is by no means a Christian nation. But these folks say America is a Christian nation. When this kind of thing happens – when the objective becomes righteousness and not good moral governance – we begin to demonise people who don't agree with us. To me that's the great malignancy in American politics. It's not new, of course, but it seems to be particularly virulent right now. I don't think they'd put up with that attitude in companies, because the governance is much more tightly focused. Yet, because of that tight focus, it does allow egomaniacal top-down management to have free rein, whereas that only goes so far in politics before you throw them out. There are shadow sides to both!

LARRY SPEARS: *Do you recall when you first discovered Greenleaf's writings and what it was you first read?*

JAMES AUTRY: I think it was in the mid to late 1980s, at the Foundation for Community Encouragement, which was Scott Peck's organisation. I met several people, and one of them – Will Clarkson was his name – first recommended Greenleaf's work to me.

LARRY SPEARS: *Can you speak briefly to your understanding of servant-leadership and what it means to you?*

JAMES AUTRY: First, understand that when I talk about servant-leadership I usually pair it – because I'm bringing it to business audiences who may have never heard of it before, who don't know The Greenleaf Center – I usually pair it with these terms: 'being useful' and 'being a resource'. The leader's responsibility, or one of them, is to ensure that the people have the resources that they need to do the work to accomplish the objectives, and the principal resource of the people is you, the leader. You have to serve the people and to think of yourself as a resource, as a servant to them. That's almost exactly the language I use when I'm talking to them.

So, I never stand up and say, "I'm going to speak now about servant-leadership." For one, I find that people who are biblically literate immediately think of the Bible, which is okay. Some, who are more literate than biblically literal, tend to think of it in ways that I don't think are particularly helpful. And others who connect it to the Bible begin to think, "Oh, it's going to be about religion." So I don't say I'm going to talk about servant-leadership. Instead I talk about leadership, and then I use what I think are the precepts of being a servant-leader.

The number one precept is, "I am here to serve, to create the community in which you can do the work that you do in order to achieve the objectives and results we are all trying to achieve together. My principal job is to serve you." What does that mean? That means, in my view, to be the kind of leader who does the five things I said before. Project authenticity and vulnerability, be present, be accepting, and see your role as being useful, as being the servant. I think it's all the techniques we talk about; it's always operating, making every decision from a basis of values, what's the right thing to do, not what's the expedient thing to do. Perhaps not even what's the most profitable thing to do, but what's the right thing to do. To me, it is a confluence of morality, which derives for the most part from my faith. Incidentally, I often find that atheists respond to the word 'spirituality'. So it's a confluence of spirituality and work.

I don't usually try to go beyond that. For one, I wouldn't know how, and two, the imperative of my work is always making myself useful to the people I'm presenting to. I don't think of myself as there to entertain them or tell them what to do, but to be helpful and useful. When people hire me, what I say to them is, "Look, I want to be useful, so I want to know what your objectives for me are." And I always say – and this is not bravado – "If at the end of it all I haven't been useful, don't pay me!" Everything I write about, everything I talk about in these books is servant-leadership, but I don't know if I can come up with a nifty, clean definition of it. But that's the general realm of vocabulary that I work in when I'm talking on these subjects. And I always recommend your books.

JOHN NOBLE: *I wanted to ask you something about your poetry, and the process of writing your poems. How much is inspiration and how much perspiration? Do you have an idea that you write a poem about, or do the words form and you write the poem?*

JAMES AUTRY: The answer is "d: all of the above"! Sometimes I get a good line and it just comes to me. Other times it's an idea, and other times it's a theme that I want to do something about that kind of percolates, percolates, percolates. It always emerges as an idea or a line. That's the inspiration part.

The greatest discovery that I made about poetry, back in the

1970s when I first started writing it, is that it yields to good crafts-manship, it yields to editing and to all the mechanics I learned as a journalist and a writer. For years I thought it just came, that it's very mystical, you get it down on paper, and you don't mess with it very much. But you do. You sometimes turn it upside down and write it in five or six different ways. I've thrown out whole sections of a poem. One of the things you learn about poetry is the least said the better. It's not about how many words you can use; it's about how few words you can use, how can you get the message, evoke the idea, the imagery, the emotion in as few words as possible.

William Faulkner once said that the most difficult thing to write is poetry, and the next most difficult is short stories. The easiest is the novel. I've never written a novel, so I've not found that to be true. I sometimes carry slips of paper around in my pocket, and I'll write lines of poetry on them and carry them around. I work on a poem and carry it in my pocket. I write my prose on a word processor, but I always write poetry by hand. There's something about the click, click, click that destroys the rhythm of the poetry, the words. I lose the rhythm of the words. So I write poetry by hand.

JOHN NOBLE: *What do you think are the poems that you've written that folk will remember you by?*

JAMES AUTRY: Well, I guess I have to choose several. The poem I'm going to be most remembered by in business is 'On Firing a Salesman'. It's been anthologised in more books in more different languages, appeared in more settings than any poem I've ever writ-ten, and I always read it because it seems to grab people. Second in the business world would be 'Threads'. The one I'll be most remem-bered for in the South comes from my first book, Nights Under a Tin Roof, and it's called 'Death in the Family'. I think in the disability community, where I've written a lot of poetry, the one I'll be most remembered for is 'Leo'.

JOHN NOBLE: *At the beginning of Love and Profit you quote Rabindranath Tagore. Has he been an influence in your work?*

JAMES AUTRY: I wouldn't say he's been an influence. It's hard to say who is and who isn't, because almost everything I read has some influence, down deep somewhere. But Tagore I admire, his work and philosophy and a lot of what he's written and said. I love the mystical poetry. I love Rumi's work very much; I'm very taken with it. His work is both love poetry and mystical spiritual poetry, and he talks about the beloved. He's often talking about God, the mystery, and the ineffable, and he mentions Jesus by name in a lot of his poetry, even though he's a Sufi poet. He writes a good deal about religion. I love Rumi's work; it is so spare.

I continue to write poetry. I've gotten back into it a lot more lately, and I've written quite a bit about my son and his autism, as well as other matters. But my work seems to be moving very much more toward the spiritual relationship with God. It's not direct. I've written a new poem called 'Death Bed Meditation'. My beloved sister-in-law died this year very suddenly from cancer, and that poem is all I really know about life that I can say in a few words.

Death Bed Meditation

All I really know about life I can say
in a few lines:
In April the small green things
will rise through the black Iowa soil
whether we're ready or not.
The Carolina wren will make her nest
in the little redwood house
my son built from a kit.
Daffodils, tulips, irises will get the attention as usual
while purslane, pig weed, and lamb's quarters
will quietly take over a place
while no one is watching.
In June the corn shoots
will etch long green lines
across the dark loamy fields
and the greenest of all green grasses
will crowd into the ditches and line the roads.

194

In August the early bloomers
begin to burn themselves out,
but in September the late yellows appear,
luring the bumblebees and yellowjackets
into a frenzy of pollination.
You already know about October,
the colour, the last burst of extravagant life.
And then all at once it seems
everything retreats, pulls into itself, rests,
and prepares for the inevitable resurrection.

JOHN NOBLE: *Is there a song or a poem, or even a line that someone else wrote that you wished you had written?*

JAMES AUTRY: Oh, gosh. You know, it's popular to say, "I wish I'd written that," or "I wish I'd said that," but it gets a little close to envy. What I'm more likely to say is I wish I could write *like* that, I wish I could achieve that sense of excellence and the ability to polish my words, find the right word, put them together in such a way to evoke the emotional response in other people that that person has evoked in me. But sure, I've said, "Gosh? I wish I'd written that sentence" about Rumi's work, the work of Yeats, and my current favourite contemporary American poet, Mary Oliver. 'The Summer Day' – now there's a poem I wish I'd had the talent to write. Genius stuff. So, yes, there are poets whose work and talent I immensely admire and I hope that I can achieve work that is of this quality.

LARRY SPEARS: *Do you have a different approach in writing poetry rather than prose? And do you have greater satisfaction in doing one or the other?*

JAMES AUTRY: I really don't. I get a great deal of satisfaction out of doing either one well. If I've crafted an essay that I think is particularly satisfying and good, I get as much satisfaction from that as I do from poetry. So I don't have a preference. Sometimes the message determines the form. I was going to write an essay about the experience of taking Communion to the shut-ins for the church. One

195

of our jobs as elders was to take it out to the shut-ins, these elderly people, and I was going to write an essay about it, but it turned into a poem almost on its own.

LARRY SPEARS: *You spent the better part of a lifetime as an editor. Did you have any kind of philosophical approach to the art of editing in a general sense that you have followed?*

JAMES AUTRY: There are certain parallels with being a manager and being an editor, in that the fundamental objective is to bring out the best of people's own work, not to impose your own work on it. That goes right back to asking the question "What would you do?" So, there's that parallel.

But I think my philosophical approach, as an editor was to do no harm, to try to find the essence of the good work there, and to help lead people to making their work the best it could be without my rewriting. it. Sometimes I've had to just go in and rewrite something because the writer was blocked, or tunnel-visioned about it, or something, but my philosophy generally was to try to see the essence of what the work was and to bring this out. Sometimes it took a little bit of fiddling, or sometimes going back and conferring with the writer, and sitting down and discussing it and having the writer redo it. But always my objective was to have the writer himself or herself bring out the best that was in there. A good editor – and I think I was a competent editor, I certainly don't think I was a great editor, on the other hand the kind of editing I was doing was not heavy literature – I think the good editor has the ability to see into that work, has to get through the words and see what's there, and then determine whether the words are adequately bringing out what is there.

Words are filters, really. Once you put a word on something, you fix it. If I say something is superb or something is good, that may mean it's superb or good, but it also means it is only that. What else is it? Put more words on it, and pretty soon you put new words on it, and then it doesn't mean anything anymore. It's nothing because it's everything, and you can't be everything. It is a constant frustration for writers to realise that words are filters. Yet we don't have another way to get the emotions of my heart into your heart, except through words. So I've got to use words, realising that they're always going to be inadequate for what I really want to achieve, but I'm trying to make them the best they can be. Oftentimes a writer falls so in love with his filters that the essence of what the writer is trying to accomplish gets mangled or camouflaged or over-filtered. The good editor will see through these filters, see what's really there, and help the writer bring it out. So my philosophy is that editing is very much like management: helping people do their best work. It's in there, look for it, give them the tools, help them, and on the rare occasions, do it for them. Sometimes I had to rewrite something. Most often it wasn't because of a writer's lack of talent, it was frustration or blockage. Who knows? Writers are like everybody else – funny creatures!

LARRY SPEARS: *What's your sense on how a leader gets better at developing a servant's heart, and how to view oneself as a servant to others?*

JAMES AUTRY: To me, the road to servanthood has to be, almost by definition, a road away from ego. I think developing the servant's heart – you know if we want to, we could shift this over to Buddhism and say 'path' of heart – that path of heart, that move to the servant's heart is a move away from ego. I think it has to be done in the context of one's own spiritual development, spiritual growth, the spiritual disciplines I mentioned before, and by reading other spiritual disciplines and picking heroes, picking people you think are the spiritual heroes, those who emulate how you would like to be, and following these models, letting them be mentors, even though they may have lived hundreds of years ago.

I think Jesus is a terrific model, but I think a lot of the interpretations of Christianity distort that model of servant-leadership. We see it manifest as judgment, manifest as trying to control people's lives, how they live, and what they believe. Here's what Jesus says to me as a role model: the strictures and structures of orthodoxy and hierarchy work against the human spirit, they work against the relationship with God, with the ultimate, with the mystery, the ineffable. And I think he said that, and lived that, over and over again, and he died for that. I like to tell the story of the Good Samaritan to people who want to listen because I want to tell it the way I really think it is, in a way I don't think biblical scholars might say it.

This person lying by the side of the road is ignored by the high priests and the church people, not because they're not compassionate people, but because the purity code prohibited even being in the same room as a dead person or touching a dead person, and you were unclean if you touched a dead person under the Hebrew purity code. Jesus was saying, "Look, you take the code so far, you lose all your compassion and connection. For fear of breaking the rule you won't even save a person's life." Along comes the Samaritan – and you know who the Samaritan would be today? The good Samaritan could be the good Communist, the good Nazi, the good Ku Klux Klan member, the good whore – whoever you perceive to be the very opposite of you. The Samaritan was the very opposite of the people Jesus was telling the story to. This is a powerful message to me about not letting the rules keep you from doing the compassionate thing, the right thing, the thing from your heart.

I think there are lots of other examples of the beatitudes being a wonderful message for us all. I think Jesus is a wonderful role model for servant-leadership, and he was a teacher. That's another thing I've left out of being a servant-leader. You don't hand down the policies; you are a good teacher and a good mentor. Jesus was a teacher. He wasn't anybody's boss. He got angry a couple of times, said some sharp things, and I think that's proof of his humanity. You could also look to the Buddha, to the prophet Mohammed, or to Moses; there are leaders and role models in all these faith traditions. My point is, whatever your faith, whatever your spiritual orientation, whatever your interest in wisdom literature, there are heroes there, there are lessons there, there are teachings there. I think you have to be active and intentional about exploring them – in the right way – not to become indoctrinated but to become educated. It's not about trying to find something to help you be a more effective leader. It's about trying to be a better person. The other will follow.

Any time people want to focus on my work, servant-leadership, or other values as a way to get better results, it's critical to start from the right place. You sincerely have to start with what you yourself are wanting to become, the being and becoming of you. To me that's what the servant's heart is about. I think it's like every other spiritual discipline or interest, I think it's all a matter of becoming. I like the scholars who say that if we really translated the first verse of the Bible, grammatically in English, it can't be done, there's no grammatical parallel. It's written in the present continuing tense, not the past tense. It's not "In the beginning God created the Heavens and the Earth." It's "In the beginning God is creating the Heavens and the Earth." It changes the whole context when you think about it that way. So I think that the path to the servant's heart is a never-ending path. You don't ever get there, but the journey is the objective.

13

Reflections:
Servant-Leadership and You

Terri McNerney

So, the very fact that you're reading this suggests to me that you are interested in servant-leadership, or at least a little curious as to what it's all about! Having read the stories so far, unless of course you've jumped straight to the end, what do you make of it all? Is it something that you would like to explore further, or develop further? Hopefully the answer is YES!

The intention of this final piece is to help you reflect on what you've learnt so far, and to decide what if anything you are going to do with it. TDIndustries started their transformation with a number of informal gatherings and conversations around the servant-leadership approach, what it meant to them and what they wanted to do with it, so I'd like to encourage you to do the same.

Some initial questions to get you thinking and exploring:

- What are the key themes that have impacted you?
- What would you like to do differently as a result?
- What do you need to get started?

If you're not quite ready for that yet, I'll share my thoughts on some of key themes of servant-leadership from the previous chapters and my own experience of some 20 years working within and without a wide range of organisations, including oil, finance, retail, media and IT. In line with the title of this book, it's about "bringing the spirit of work to work". These themes will overlap to some extent, as all are part of the greater whole.

Servant first, then leader

This is very much about each of us having a strong sense of what it is we want to contribute to the world, what it is we want to do with our lives, understanding what is it that really matters to us, what you are passionate about, so that from this place we can lead others to help make it happen.

Over the years I've found people have very different reactions to the word 'passion', so how do *you* respond to it? Some leaders love it, are visibly energetic and are happy to show their strength of feeling. Others dislike the word, and believe it has no place in the work environment. Then there are the leaders who are uncomfortable with the expectations that seem to go with the word, preferring a less obvious way.

We often judge others based on our own preferences, so maybe it's time to inquire further and find out what really matters to others around you and how you can tap into this hidden reservoir. There may be people around you who have intensely strong feelings about certain things, but don't necessarily show it and you may be one of them.

In relation to whichever context makes most sense to you, be it in home, work, the bigger world...based on James Autry suggestions, think about the following:

- What is your purpose? What it is that you really want to achieve?
- What are you passionate about? What drives you?
- What really matters to you?

Once you can get clear on your answers to the above, you should have identified a few areas in which you really want to contribute, to serve others. Then again, it may be that you are more inwardly focused, and have more you want to achieve for yourself.

Sometimes, we need to serve ourselves first before we can serve others. A great, often quoted example, is of the safety instructions on an airplane. When the oxygen masks come down, "make sure you put your own on first before you see to the needs of others" as obviously you'll be of no use to anyone collapsed in a heap.

As with the idea of "leadership from the inside out", we have to be able to lead ourselves first before we can lead others. So do you trust yourself? Are you honest with yourself? Do you keep your own commitments? If not, it's going to be hard to do this for others! Being a servant-leader is ultimately about serving a need greater than your own, so are you ready for that?

- Do you need to serve yourself first?
- Are you ready to serve others?
- What do you want to take the lead on?

Playing to your strengths

We all have skills and strengths that are particular to us, our natural talents if you like, some realised, others not. How often do you and your colleagues get a chance to put these to good use, to show what you can really do, to make a great contribution? And, to do so easily, without lots of stress and strain? Many of us can get caught up in the ever-increasing demands on our time. However it's more about "managing our energy not our time", and ensuring we have sufficient energy for the things that matter most in our lives. When we're doing things we love, that come easily to us, they take far less energy than when doing things that feel difficult, complicated, and not within our natural skill range. As a leader, and in particular a servant-leader, it's about using your talents in service of others and in service of something greater than yourself.

When working with a Finance team recently, we spent some time exploring their strengths and passions, and even though they'd been working together for a few years, because of the constant focus on getting the work done they hadn't realised some of the hidden talents within the team. They'd had a lot of challenges with PC systems and databases, and this was getting in the way of achieving certain targets. Through this conversation, it became apparent that one of the team had a passion and a talent for this area but because it wasn't part of his current responsibilities, he'd never thought to volunteer this information. By the end of the workshop, various responsibilities were re-assigned in line with people's interests. A few months later, this person was promoted and is surprising everyone, including himself, with his achievements.

- What do you love doing?
- What do you feel strongly about?
- What comes easily and naturally to you?
- Do you take the opportunity to use these talents to the benefit of others?
- How can you use these talents to support others?
- What takes up most of your energy?
- Is there someone else better suited to doing this?
- Can you delegate this to someone else who has a talent for it?

Do those served ...grow?

This is probably one of the most obvious and easy to understand and, as Robert Greenleaf said, "the best test".

A Finance leader when exploring leadership competencies, asked me: "Do you mean to tell me that if lots of my people keep making the same mistakes I should train them?" She was genuinely shocked. She'd always assumed that they were stupid and just didn't get it. The idea that it was her role to coach and develop these people, so they could learn and grow, had never entered her head. And as we explored it further it became apparent that she'd never been trained or coached herself; she'd had to learn it the hard way – and so should they!

Time and time again I find leaders saying how surprised they are at the creativity and great ideas generated by their team, once they're given some space and encouragement.

- So have you experienced good coaching and development?
- Do you provide this for your people?
- Do you make assumptions about other's ability?

- Is it worth checking this out?
- Do you give your people the necessary space and encouragement they need to do a great job?

Support and challenge

We all know about the increasing numbers of challenges that we seem to be faced with on a daily basis. The question is how much support do you get, and do you give to others, in order to ensure the best possible outcomes? High performance results from a combination of high challenge and high support. When there is little support, you get stress not high performance.

When working with a worldwide team of engineers a few years ago, the question of noticing the warning signs of when things are getting to overload came up. The leader told the following story. "I was out for dinner with some friends the other Saturday, and when I got up, I went to take my seat belt off! At that point I realised I'd been spending too much time on planes recently!"

When a leader is this overloaded, it's unlikely that they have anything left for their team or organisation, never mind themselves!

- Where are you right now? High performance or stress?
- Where is your team?
- What can you do to serve them, provide them with the support and resources they need to do a great job?
- How can you best serve yourself, identify what support you need and how you might get it?

Guiding principles and core values – espoused v actual

Servant-leadership is very much a values-based approach, and so defining your core values, your guiding principles as an organisation, as a team, and then working to them, is key – so that whatever the situation, no matter how difficult things get, you have some clear guidelines to help see you through.

In my early years as a consultant, I went to visit a senior leader within a large multinational, with a colleague of mine. We'd been asked in by someone who'd been there a few months and was increasingly frustrated by the lack of process in place to help him achieve what he was assigned to do. He suggested we meet with his boss to discuss how we could help. As we began the initial inquiry, the boss proudly told us about all the wonderful processes that were in place. He looked at me and said. "You seem confused – didn't you know?" I felt uncomfortable and wondered if it was all a mistake, and then I asked him, "And how well do these processes work in practice, day to day?"

"Ah," he said after a few moments, "that's a very different question."

And I often find the same thing with company values – the plaque on the wall saying wonderful things and the day-to-day behaviours revealing something entirely different.

An older man was talking about a younger man and saying, "The trouble with youngsters today is that they don't have any values!" Someone else replied, "They do – they're just different to yours."

- How clear are you on the core values of your company?
- How well do they reflect the day-to-day ways of being and doing within your organisation?
- In times of crisis how well do these values guide you?
- Are the company values in line with your own values?

Diversity & inclusion

A company decided to increase the diversity of its workforce, by bringing in people from a wider range of backgrounds than previously. Over the next few months it became apparent that two of the new recruits did not appear to be fitting in, and there were various examples of them upsetting people. They had come from a very different industry and culture and had not been helped in any way to adapt. They were left to get on with it, on the basis that diversity was a good thing.

I was asked if I could help by providing coaching, which I did. I had worked in the two industries and was aware of just how differently people operated within each, and it was no wonder they were struggling!

Culture is often an unseen thing, an unspoken thing, something you can only see once you leave that particular environment and so in terms of diversity, less visible than some other differences. And it can have a huge impact on new people joining a company.

> *"It's only when we understand what we have in common that we can begin to appreciate our differences."*
>
> Clarissa Pinkola Estes[36]

So So for me it's about ensuring there is an alignment around the values of the company and the individual and that this is explored in depth during the recruitment phase. Once this foundation is agreed, then you can appreciate the differences that people have to offer.

- How well you do explore people's values during the recruitment phase?
- What support do you provide for people once they join your organisation?
- Do you support people is finding out how things work around here?
- Do you value the differences people have to offer?

Role-modelling servant-leadership – enacting

Saying one thing and then doing another undermines you as a leader. Trust comes from consistency of action amongst other things, and so people will be looking to see if you really mean what you say and act accordingly, or if it's just a matter of saying the words because they sound good. Communication is only 7% words. The rest is a combination of tonality and body language, so when you are

---

[36] Clarissa Pinkola Estes, *Women Who Run With Wolves: Contacting the Power of the Wild Woman*, Rider, 1992

communicating, you're communicating with your whole being, not just your mouth! If you say one thing and communicate another, people will stop believing you over time and the trust will go.

So often during change in organisations, I hear leaders saying that they have to wait before they have all the facts before they can tell people what's happening, and all the time the rumour mill is at work with all sorts of stories being created as to what's happening. If a space is left, people will fill it with their own versions.

If you trust people with the truth you will most likely get much more involved and engaged employees. During the 9/11 crisis Southwest Airlines told everyone that same morning that they had a job, and not to worry. This then allowed a very motivated workforce to start contacting all their customers that same afternoon and send them a refund. The employees helped to save the company. Southwest Airlines is now one of the biggest and most successful airlines in the world.

How often have you been part of a leadership team which makes an agreement at a meeting, only to afterwards have various leaders saying completely different things outside the meeting? How much trust can this generate when the leaders don't even agree?

A servant-leadership team will work to a core set of values, challenge ideas, speak openly and honestly and then once a decision is agreed, stick by it and support their colleagues. They set an example for the rest of the organisation, being a role model for servant-leadership.

- Do you find yourself saying one thing and meaning another?
- How well do you fight for your beliefs in meetings?
- Once a decision is made are you willing to stand by it and support it?
- If decisions go against your values, what do you do?
- How aligned are you as a leadership team?

Clarifying the intention of conversations

It can save a lot of frustration and allow a lot more individual growth, if you can clarify the intent behind a conversation upfront. Often a leader can feel the need to save time by telling a person what to do. The servant-leader will take more time to help the person explore the options for themselves and so grow and develop as a consequence.

Years back when I was working within a organisation, I had a particular challenge I was working on and felt in need of some support, so I went to my boss and started to explain where I was with the project. Before I could make clear what it was that I wanted, he went off into a 15-minute description of everything he knew about the project. I remember thinking, "I know that, yah, yah," and feeling quite frustrated.

On reflection, what I realised I needed was someone to ask me a few questions to help me think things through and get clearer as to what I could do next. Instead I got a download of data, most of which I'd found out already, and a decision as to how to proceed.

- How often do you tell people what to do?
- Do you take the time to help people explore the options for themselves?

Strategy and culture: the soft stuff is the hard stuff

As Colleen Barrett, President of Southwest Airlines says, "Culture eats strategy."

Culture is often described simply as "the way we do things round here." Understanding the impact of change on your culture, your people and how you can best support them through this is a key role of the servant-leader.

One leader I worked with expressed his huge frustration, having written the strategy for a particular business, only to find that now that they were moving on to how to implement it, all sorts of issues and resistance was happening. He seemed to think that the hard part was writing the strategy paper and the rest was easy. Challenging as it is to write a good strategy paper, the really hard part is usually implementing the strategy and making it part of day-to-day practice. In my experience, this is often the piece that is underestimated by leaders and not given the attention it deserves. Bringing people with you takes time and a strong leadership team leading the way.

As a consequence, even though the new structures are in place, and the new systems have been implemented, somehow the people aren't working the way they should with the new ways. Why is this? Often it is because they are still in the mindset of the old ways; they are still continuing the old culture, and if no attention is given to this area, it can continue for years. Just look at a number of mergers where the integration has never fully taken place as far as the people are concerned.

- How much value do you put on the cultural issues v the strategic issues?
- Have your people been given the opportunity to contribute their ideas, or has it been done to them?
- Do you spend time understanding where your people are, so you can help them adapt to the new ways of working?
- As a leadership team have you changed your ways and set an example.
- Do people know what's expected of them in the new world?
- Have they been given the necessary support and training to work with the new ways?

Honest feedback – tough love (as TDIndustries calls it)

So this is where the servant-leadership approach can be tough! It's about respecting people enough to tell them the truth, and to work with them and support them, so they can grow and develop. It's about setting standards and holding people to them and if after a reasonable amount of effort on both sides, it's not going to work, it's again being honest about this and finding a way to support the person to move onto something more suitable for them.

Often in organisations this is one of the most common challenges

I come across. No matter how experienced or inexperienced the leaders, time and time again the question of how to give effective and timely feedback comes up. In many cases it has been avoided for years, with "problem people" simply moved around from department to department, or, worst still, promoted, because no one can find a way to be honest with them and tell them what is not working! How is this serving these people? How it is serving the organisation? Obviously it's not.

It leaves the "problem people" with the impression that they are doing a great job, with lots of moves and promotions, and then many years later when some leader is courageous enough to deal with the situation, the employee is dumbfounded and often destroyed, because no-one has ever told them this before! The organisation has spent a lot of time and energy over the years working around these people, when they could have been putting that precious time and energy to better use and serving both themselves and the employees at the same time. It's a question of skill and training as well as the courage to deal with the situation. And I believe, if faced early on, it's much less of a challenge than if left for year and years!

- Do you feel able to give honest feedback in a way that enables the person to grow?
- What support do you need to do this?

And in conclusion

So hopefully you have a few things to be thinking about and some ideas as to how to get started. Servant-leadership does not come in a ready-made package that you implement and then move onto the next thing. It is a philosophy – a way of being and behaving that underpins everything that you do. It provides a strong foundation upon which many a successful business and organisation has been built. The focus then for each organisation is on finding a way that works best for you. Sometimes it can be the little things that each of us do that makes the difference, to our own and others' experience. Other times, the ways of being and behaving are so ingrained in the culture that it can take a much longer time to turn things around.

Robert Greenleaf's book *Servant Leadership*: *A Journey into the Nature of Legitimate Power & Greatness*[37], has inspired many of today's writers on leadership, including Warren Bennis, Margaret Wheatley, Peter Senge and Stephen Covey, to name a few. In this respect, many of the ideas may seem familiar to you – or not...

Whatever your situation, if you've read this far, then I would encourage you to find something that really matters to you, something that is bigger than yourself, and from that place, lead. That's what servant-leadership is all about. So...

- What are you going to do next?
- How can we serve each other?

---

[37] Robert K. Greenleaf, *Servant-Leadership: A Journey Into the Nature of Legitimate Power and Greatness*, Paulist Press, 2002

Appendix 1
The Greenleaf Centre (UK)

The Greenleaf Centre UK was founded in November 1997. Its mission is to help improve the caring and quality of all institutions through an approach to leadership and organisational structure that emphasises increased service to others, a holistic approach to work, promoting a sense of community and the wider sharing of power in decision-making in the workplace.

It is committed to spreading the concepts and philosophy of Robert Greenleaf's vision of servant-leadership.

It aims to do this in a way that invites people to work as and be servant-leaders, through the Centre serving their needs and helping them grow.

We do this by:

- Acting as a Centre for servant-leadership resources
- Running annual conferences where those interested in servant-leadership can come to share their experiences and learn from each other
- Running regional conferences as and when the demand is there
- Providing speakers for leadership and other conferences on servant-leadership
- Helping those in education, especially in leadership, bring servant-leadership into their subject
- Talking to leaders and managers in industry and other organisations about their issues, and whether servant-leadership is appropriate for them
- Offering small group discussions for support on servant-leadership applications
- Running workshops on servant-leadership – "The Leader's Journey"

- Writing articles for newspapers and journals on servant-leadership
- Offering help and speaking at international conferences – e.g. Australia, South Africa, USA

For news and updates please see:
www.greenleaf.org.uk
http://www.servantleadership.org.uk